Overleaf: Staffordshire Bull Terrier photographed by Paulette Braun.

Opposite Page: Staffordshire Bull Terrier photographed by Isabelle Francais.

The Publisher would like to thank the owners of the dogs in this book, including: Elinda Anderson, Joseph D. Arcuri, Dianna Caulk, Dennis Flynn, Anthony D. George, Bonnie Gottier, Jean Greco, Ramona Guerrera, Julie King, Ann Lettis, Chris Petrasek, Rachel Redsun, Harry Rodeheaver, Irma Tillman.

Photographers: Elinda Anderson, Paulette Braun, Wil de Veer, Isabelle Francais, Dayna Lemke, Robert Smith, Tien Tran Photography

The author acknowledges the contribution of Judy Iby to the following chapters: Health Care, Sport of Purebred Dogs, Identification and Finding the Lost Dog, Traveling with Your Dog, and Behavior and Canine Communication.

The portrayal of canine pet products in this book is for general instructive value only; the appearance of such products does not necessarily constitute an endorsement by the authors, the publisher, or the owners of the dogs portrayed in this book.

The author would like to thank Ann Lettis and Karen Lau for contributions about BSL.

© Copyright T.F.H. Publications, Inc.

Distributed in the UNITED STATES to the Pet Trade by T.F.H. Publications, Inc., 1 TFH Plaza, Neptune City, NJ 07753; on the Internet at www.tfh.com; in CANADA by Rolf C. Hagen Inc., 3225 Sartelon St., Montreal, Quebec H4R 1E8; Pet Trade by H & L Pet Supplies Inc., 27 Kingston Crescent, Kitchener, Ontario N2B 2T6; in ENGLAND by T.F.H. Publications, PO Box 74, Havant PO9 5TT; in AUSTRALIA AND THE SOUTH PACIFIC by T.F.H. (Australia), Pty. Ltd., Box 149, Brookvale 2100 N.S.W., Australia; in NEW ZEALAND by Brooklands Aquarium Ltd., 5 McGiven Drive, New Plymouth, RD1 New Zealand; in SOUTH AFRICA by Rolf C. Hagen S.A. (PTY.) LTD., P.O. Box 201199, Durban North 4016, South Africa; in JAPAN by T.F.H. Publications. Published by T.F.H. Publications, Inc.

A NEW OWNER'S GUIDE TO
STAFFORDSHIRE BULL TERRIERS

DAYNA LEMKE

Contents

2000 Edition

The Staffordshire should convey strength, as well as sound body and temperament.

An affectionate dog, the Staffordshire Bull Terrier makes a great companion.

The Staffordshire Bull Terrier is a "people" dog and is happiest in the company of his family.

The Staffordshire is a graceful and athletic dog that can be trained to compete in many activities.

Staffordshire puppies need a lot of love, care, and training to develop into good canine citizens.

HISTORY and Origin of the Staffordshire Bull Terrier

I t has been written " . . . and, indeed, there is scarcely any task to which a dog of his size may be set that he will not execute as well as, or better than, most others. He will learn tricks with the poodle, fetch and carry with the Newfoundland—take water with that dog, though his coat will not suffer him to remain in so long—hunt with the spaniel and fight 'til all's blue. For thorough gameness, united with obedience, good temper, and intelligence, he surpasses any breed in existence."

Stonehenge
On British Dogs, 1888
Stonehenge was the pen name taken by the brilliant 19th century English dog authority, J.

The Staffordshire Bull Terrier is believed to have originated from three English breeds—the English Staffordshire, the English White Terrier, and the Manchester Terrier.

H. Walsh. It is obvious from what he wrote that the gentleman was more than a bit impressed with the bull-and-terrier cross that was so popular in his day, and there should be no surprise about Stonehenge's glowing superlatives. The dogs he wrote of were believed to be the result of crossing three of England's most outstanding and highly regarded home products—the English Staffordshire, the English White Terrier, and the Manchester Terrier. The combination produced a general classification of dogs that was commonly referred to as the bull and terrier or Pit Bull. Those who owned these dogs believed they far surpassed the best of any of their progenitors.

From this general classification, there emerged two distinct types of bull-and-terrier dogs. A certain Mr. James Hinks paid homage to his aristocratic upbringing by producing the elegant-looking animal we now know as the "White Cavalier," registered by the kennel clubs of the world as the Bull Terrier. He accomplished this by crossing the existing Pit Bull with the now extinct English White Terrier, among other breeds.

This accounted for what might be referred to as the "wealthy man's" bull terrier, but there were far more of these dogs that lived with and loved the common man. There is no doubt whatsoever that it is from the latter group that the dog

The Staffordshire has long held a reputation as being a tenacious guard dog and loyal companion.

we now know as the Staffordshire Bull Terrier emerged.

These dogs were all things to their people. They stood guard against intruders, kept the premises vermin-free, served as nannies for the children, and, sadly, even provided entertainment for some in the form of dog fighting.

In order to understand where these bull-and-terrier dogs came by the endearing characteristics that they maintain to this day, we must have at least a working knowledge of the origin and purpose of the Staffordshire and their terrier ancestors. To do so, we must take a giant step back into time to the very source of every canine breed that exists today—the ancient ancestor, *Canis lupus*, the wolf. The road from the wolf in the wild to the Staffordshire Bull Terrier lounging on your sofa is extremely long and just as fascinating.

The amount of time that it took for the wolf to move out of the forest and into man's cave dwellings is a point of conjecture. However, it seems obvious that observation of the wolf could easily have taught prehistoric man some effective hunting techniques that he would be able to use advantageously. Also, many of the wolf's social habits might have seemed strikingly familiar to early man. The association grew from there.

The ancestors of the Staffordshire descended from the ancient mastiff breeds and were often used as warrior dogs due to their formidable size and imposing nature.

The wolves that could assist in satisfying the unending human need for food were, of course, most highly prized. It also became increasingly obvious as the man-wolf relationship developed through the ages that certain descendants of these increasingly domesticated wolves could also be used by man to assist in survival pursuits other than hunting. Those wolves that were large enough and aggressive enough to protect man and the tribe he lived with from danger were also highly valued.

In their enlightening study of the development of the dog breeds, *The Natural History of Dogs*, Richard and Alice Feinnes classify most dogs as having descended from one of four major groups: the Northern group, the Dingo group, the Greyhound group, and the Mastiff group. Each of these groups traces back to separate and distinct branches of the wolf family.

The two groups that directly affect the development of the bull-and-terrier breeds are the Mastiff and Arctic classifications. The "bull" ancestors of the Staffordshire Bull Terrier descended from the Mastiff group. This group owes its primary heritage to

9

the Tibetan wolf (*Canis lupus chanco* or *laniger*). The great diversity of the dogs included in this group indicate that they are not entirely of pure blood, because the specific breeds included have undoubtedly been influenced by descendants of the other three groups.

The Arctic or Nordic group of dogs is a direct descendant of the rugged northern wolf. Included in the many breeds of this group are Alaskan Malamutes, Chows, German Shepherds, and the much smaller Welsh Corgis and Spitz-type dogs. This group also includes the early terriers.

The Staffordshire's terrier heritage has contributed to his compact build, high intelligence, and aggressive personality.

DEVELOPMENT OF THE STAFFORDSHIRE

The tribes that occupied northern Europe were known to have kept large, fierce dogs of the Mastiff type. The Romans bred these Mastiff-type dogs to fight in the arena against bulls, bears, and other wild animals. The latter were known until the Middle Ages as Alains or Alaunts. In Britain, these same large and fierce dogs became known as bandogs because ropes, chains, or bands were employed to keep them under control.

The ferocious forerunners of today's bull breeds were brought about through manipulative breeding in England of these Alaunt or Mastiff-type dogs. Their original purpose was to assist butchers in controlling the savage bulls from which food for the table would be gleaned. It was also believed that the meat from bulls that had been "worried" by these bandogs prior to butchering was much more tender and nutritious than meat that came from bulls immediately slaughtered.

The dogs were developed to have short legs and heavy bodies, which served them in keeping out of the way of the bulls' horns. It does not tax the imagination to see how readily this functional animal could be adapted to salve man's perverse nature in cruel sport. Eventually, dogs were pitted against bulls

Once used in the sport of bullbaiting, which was outlawed in 1835, the Staffordshire was often forced to fight bulls as well as other dogs.

to see who owned the most ferocious dog, the dog most capable of bringing the bull to the ground. Thus, was born the sport of "bull-baiting."

Just prior to the end of the 1800s, Hugh Dalziel, a noted dog writer of that era, wrote: "When the rules of bull-baiting became consolidated, and the chief point was for the dog to run in farthest and fairest, tackling the bull in front, dogs would be selected and bred of low and strong formation."

THE TERRIER EVOLVES

While the Bulldog forerunners were undergoing their permutation, another transformation was taking place. There was a small spitz-type dog somewhat resembling a small elkhound that was used by the Neolithic pile dwelling people to follow and confront foxes and badgers in their holes. The lithe build, aggressive nature, and lightning responses of these dogs made them particularly suitable for hunting small vermin.

Many new breeds were developed, both from this original source and through crosses with other breeds already in existence—among them the terrier breeds. Interestingly, most of the original terrier breeds were developed in Europe and even more specifically, in England, Scotland, and Ireland. Although countless varieties of long- and short-legged terrier dogs evolved, it is believed the earliest terriers were black and tan and had a wire-type coat.

The Staffordshire developed when breeders combined the stamina and courage of the mastiff breeds with the tenacity of the terriers from the British Isles.

At any rate, these terrier dogs retained the mercurial nature and lightning speed of their Spitz ancestors. This did not escape the notice of the proponents of the cruel but highly popular bull-baiting events that existed

The Staffordshire Bull Terrier derived his name from the English county of Stafford, where the breed had a reputation as an irrepressible fighting dog.

in England from 1209 until 1835, when the pastime was outlawed.

In order to provide more "action" for the spectators, breeders of the bull-baiting dogs looked toward a smaller, more athletic dog than the cumbersome bulldog. The bulldog was inclined to clamp his jaws onto the bull's nose and hang on until either the bull succumbed or the dog himself was bashed into unconsciousness on the ground. The tenacity of this approach was praiseworthy, but provided little "entertainment" value.

A source of the sought-after "action" was found in the terrier breeds. Combining the blood of the terriers with that of the bulldog resulted in a dog that was strong and tenacious but also possessed lightning speed and trigger-quick reactions. Thus, was born the bull-and-terrier cross, or as the resulting dogs were to become known, the Bull Terriers.

As an adjunct to the barbarous bull-baiting events, dog fights were staged, and when bull-baiting was abolished in 1835, dog fighting, though equally illegal, flourished. The reason for the continuance and the increase in popularity of the dog fights was quite frankly that dogs were portable and easily hidden from the authorities, and dog fights could be easily ended and disbursed in the event of police raids.

None were better at these barbaric events than the bull-and-terrier crosses and particularly the working man's bull and terrier—the dog that was eventually to become known as the

Known for his devotion to his master, the Staffordshire's eagerness to please and protective instincts make him a loyal family pet.

Staffordshire Bull Terrier. The Staffordshire name was given to the dogs because a good many of these fighting dogs came from the area in and around the English county of Stafford.

The dogs were ready, willing, and able to do almost anything that their master asked. They were very devoted to their families. In fact, it amazes today's dog fancier to realize that the same dogs that were maniacal fighters in the pit would go home the same night to baby-sit the family's children.

BEAUTY AND BRAINS

By the 1930s, English dog fanciers were paying as much attention to what their dogs looked like as they were to their origin and purpose. Prior to 1935, only the white Bull Terrier had been recognized by The Kennel Club of England, but in that year, those who owned the "other" Bull Terriers came together to form the first Staffordshire Bull Terrier Club under the leadership of its president, Jack Barnard. A standard was drawn up at this time, and by 1938, the fanciers of the breed celebrated the awarding of the first championship points at the Birmingham dog show.

It was only months later that the first champions in the breed were made—Joe Mallen's Gentleman Jim was the first male champion and Joe Dunn's Lady Eve became the first female champion.

Many Staffordshire Bull Terriers came to America with their immigrating families, and they were recognized as a separate breed by the AKC in 1975.

THE STAFFORD IN AMERICA

Between the mid-1800s and 1950, many bull-and-terrier breeds came to America with their immigrating owners. Most of these dogs lived out their lives as companions, but there is little doubt that an unfortunate number of the dogs were also put in the fighting pits of this new country as well. Because there was no organized club to take inventory of how many of these dogs existed within the confines of the US, not much can be said of their influence. However, in 1960, a nucleus of Stafford owners in California directed their energies toward legitimizing their breed in America.

Their efforts were repaid in 1975 when the Staffordshire Bull Terrier was given official recognition in the American Kennel Club (AKC). The first dog to be registered with the AKC was the English import, Champion Tinkinswood Imperial, and the first champion to be recorded by the AKC was the Australian import, Becky Northwark Sharpe.

CHARACTERISTICS

The Staffordshire Bull Terrier is extremely fortunate in that it is not, nor will ever be, what can be considered a glamorous breed. A good Stafford certainly cannot be described as beautiful in the conventional sense of the word. Many breeds, including the Staffordshire Bull Terrier, are absolutely irresistible as puppies. Stafford puppies are best described as an acquired taste. (But once that taste is acquired, they become an addiction!) The Stafford waits for the person who has been previously introduced to the breed and who is aware that the breed matures into a splendid companion—arguably one of the best companion breeds in the canine world.

With all of this said, buying a dog, especially a puppy, before being absolutely sure you want to make that commitment can be a serious mistake. The prospective

Make sure that everyone in the family is ready to take on the responsibility of caring for a new Staffordshire puppy before taking one home.

16

Although the Staffordshire is known as an all-purpose breed, it is important to make sure that the puppy you choose will fit in with your lifestyle and personality. dog owner must clearly understand the amount of time and work involved in dog ownership. Failure to understand the extent of commitment that dog ownership involves is one of the primary reasons so many unwanted canines end their lives in an animal shelter.

Before anyone contemplates the purchase of a dog, there are some very important conditions that must be considered. One of the first important questions that must be answered is whether or not the person who will ultimately be responsible for the dog's care and well-being actually wants a dog.

All too often it is the mother of the household, even working mothers, who must shoulder the responsibility of the family dog's day-to-day care. While the children in the family, perhaps even the father, may be wildly enthusiastic about having a dog, it must be remembered they are away most of the day at school or at work. It is often Mom who will be taking on the additional responsibility of primary caregiver for the family dog.

Pets are a wonderful method of teaching children responsibility, but it should be remembered that the enthusiasm that inspires children to promise anything in order to have a new puppy may quickly wane. Who will take care of the puppy once the novelty wears off? Does that person want a dog?

The desire to own a dog aside, does the lifestyle of the family actually provide for responsible dog ownership? If the entire family is away from home from early morning to late at night, who will provide for all of the puppy's needs? Feeding, exercise, outdoor access, and the like cannot be provided if no one is home.

Another important factor to consider is whether or not the breed of dog is suitable for the person or the family with which he will be living. Some breeds can handle the rough-and-tumble play of young children. Some cannot. On the other hand, some dogs are so large and clumsy, especially as puppies, that they could easily and unintentionally injure an infant.

Then, too, there is the matter of grooming. A luxuriously coated dog is certainly beautiful to behold, but all that hair takes a great deal of care. At first thought, it would seem that a smooth-coated dog like the Staffordshire would eliminate this problem. As we will see, this is not so. While there is no long hair to contend with, there is a great deal that the Staffordshire owner is called upon to do in the way of skin care and cleanliness if he or she wants a happy, healthy pet.

As great as claims are for any breed's intelligence and trainability, remember that the new dog must be taught every household rule that he is to observe. Some dogs catch on more quickly than others, and puppies are just as inclined to forget or disregard lessons as young human children.

CASE FOR THE PUREBRED DOG

Just about all puppies are sweet and cuddly, but not all puppies grow up to be the picture of what we find attractive. What is considered beautiful by one person is not necessarily seen as so by another. It is almost impossible to determine what a mixed-breed puppy will look like as an adult, nor will it be possible to determine if the mixed-breed puppy's temperament is suitable for the person or family who wishes to own him. If the puppy grows up to be too big, too stubborn, or too active for the owner, what then will happen to him?

Size and temperature can vary to a degree, even within a purebred breed. Still, selective breeding over many generations has produced dogs that give the would-be owner a reasonable assurance of what the purebred puppy will look and act like as an adult. Points of attractiveness completely aside, this predictability is more important than one might think.

A person who wants a dog to go along on those morning jogs or long-distance runs is not going to be particularly happy with a short-nosed, lethargic breed like a Bulldog. Nor is the fastidious housekeeper, whose picture of the ideal dog is one that lies quietly at the feet of his master by the hour and never sheds, going to be particularly happy with a huge, shaggy dog with the temperament of a whirling dervish.

Your Stafford puppy should grow up to look and act a lot like his parents. Int/Am. Ch. Slam Dance, CGC, with son Day Dream Pistols at Dawn.

Purebred puppies will grow up to look like their adult relatives and, by and large, they will behave pretty much like the rest of their family. Any dog, mixed breed or not, has the potential to be a loving companion. However, a purebred dog offers reasonable assurance

that he will not only suit the owner's lifestyle but the person's aesthetic demands as well.

WHO SHOULD OWN A STAFFORDSHIRE BULL TERRIER?

What kind of a person should own a Staffordshire? As much as we love and cherish these dogs, they are not the dog for everyone. There are many special considerations that must be taken into account before the decision to own a Staffordshire is made. It must be remembered that one is dealing with a breed that is "blessed" with a combination of the wily thinking ability of a terrier and the determination to follow through of a Bulldog.

Staffords are housedogs: First and foremost, the Staffordshire is a people dog. The breed is not suited to being isolated from the people it loves, nor can the short-coated Stafford withstand weather extremes. Severe cold and heat could cost a Stafford his life.

Secured yards are necessary: Staffordshires are loyal but easily bored. The Stafford is an active dog, and boredom can take even the most devoted dog over and under fences that would stump most other breeds. Staffordshires love people, and they are not adverse to accepting an invitation to take a stroll with a passing child or hop into the car of a total stranger. For this reason, the Staffordshire owner must have a securely fenced yard.

No unfenced swimming pools: The average Staffordshire is only a middle-class swimmer, but he does love the water. There have been accidents, even where pools have been completely fenced in because someone inadvertently left the gate open. You must be sure that your Stafford can swim if the dog is going to be anywhere near your pool, and you must be sure he knows how and where to get out of the pool.

No one who wants a "macho" or aggressive dog need apply: A home that encourages aggressive behavior is not the home for a Staffordshire. A Staffordshire that is goaded into a fight is something you do not want to see!

The Staffordshire Bull Terrier is a "people" dog—he is happiest when in the company of his family.

No indiscriminate breeding: It takes a long time to understand what kind of stock is even suitable for breeding and an even longer time to learn the intricacies of breeding, whelping, and rearing a litter of Staffordshires. Also,

Gentle and dignified, the Staffordshire Bull Terrier gets along great with other animals. Dolly and Dozer, owned by Elinda Anderson.

there are not hundreds of homes just waiting for Stafford puppies. Leave the breeding to breeders!

The Staffordshire is a docile, affectionate companion and yet, will be playful and active if you want him to be. The breed is absolutely wonderful with children and the elderly. Their special talent in life is providing companionship. Few breeds have the same degree of talent for companionship that is possessed by the Staffordshire. A Staffordshire may not give two hoots about guarding a missile site, but watch him take care of a toddler as the two amble along, with the child holding steadfastly to the collar (or ear, for that matter!).

The Staffordshire's forbidding reputation works for and against him. People who do not know the breed are usually inclined to step around or away from the Stafford, because they've heard stories of those "pit" dogs. This makes the Stafford a good watchdog without exerting any effort.

While Staffordshires can be tough with other aggressive dogs, their humans are their lives and, when raised with other animals, they can make delightful buddies. I know of Staffords that play with parrots, rabbits, and even pot-belly pigs! My own love their cats. They are clowns and will do things just to make you laugh. They are also very sensitive to your moods and will sympathize with you, rejoice with you, and be still or grieve with you.

The energetic and tolerant Staffordshire makes a great playmate and natural babysitter for children. This Staffordshire gets a big hug from his friend.

Staffordshires are gentle and dignified. Part of their charm is that they look so tough, but they really aren't at all. Their inner beauty will steal your heart. When it comes to their humans, Staffordshires are totally forgiving and totally loving. They are true companions in every sense of the word.

A Stafford can be stubborn, however. Do not forget that determined Bulldog heritage. Even so, you must be fair and consistent in training, because the breed is extremely sensitive. They are very sensitive to voice tones, and firm voice correction will do wonders.

Some Staffords are a bit harder in temperament than others, and when these dogs are older, they will accept a bit more correction. However, none of them can tolerate treatment that is in the least bit abusive. Staffords are often pouters and are masters at showing you exactly how they feel about being scolded. They are very sensitive to their person's moods and even capable of reading their minds when they are closely bonded.

BREED-SPECIFIC LEGISLATION

Those interested in owning a Staffordshire Bull Terrier should be aware that breed-specific legislation and dog control bylaws have been enacted in some cities in Canada, and there are attempts being made to enact similar legislation in some sections of the United States.

If you live in Canada and you own a beautiful Staffordshire Bull Terrier, one of the first things you will notice is that most of your neighbors and the public will identify your dog as a Pit Bull, due to the bad press coverage that exists in North America.

Some areas have breed-specific legislation that may affect your Staffordshire Bull Terrier. Educate yourself and take the necessary precautions to keep your dog safe.

As a potential or new Stafford owner, you will need to go to your nearest municipal (city) hall to obtain a copy of your local dog control bylaws. Familiarize yourself fully with these laws, as not all cities in Canada have breed-specific dog control bylaws. Unfortunately, many Canadian cities have breed-specific type bylaws, which usually single out the American Pit Bull Terrier, the American Staffordshire Terrier, Staffordshire Bull Terrier, and a category of crossbreeds of these dog breeds. What this usually means is that your dog, by virtue of his breed, will be classified as a dangerous dog. You may have to pay a higher annual licensing fee and/or face other restrictions as stipulated by the local dangerous dog bylaw.

Besides educating yourself thoroughly about the breed you have chosen to own, you will need to educate other immediate family members and close friends about how the dog control

Be sure to introduce your Staffordshire to others and educate them on the positive aspects of owning this amiable, trustworthy breed.

bylaws impact your Stafford. As you raise, train, socialize, and exercise your dog, it is very important for you to be alert and aware of the other dogs around you. It may not be your dog that will misbehave, but as a responsible Stafford owner, it is necessary for you to be absolutely sure of the safety of your surrounding environment before you allow your dog off leash anywhere.

If you need more information on how you can change breed-specific dog control bylaws in your area, contact your local dog clubs or breed organizations and search the Internet web sites that pertain to this subject. Please remember that positive change first begins at home, so try your best to be well informed and to let others know about the wonderful breed of dog you have chosen to own as a family member.

STANDARD for the Staffordshire Bull Terrier

The American Kennel Club standard for the Staffordshire is written in simple, straightforward language that can be read and understood by even the beginning fancier. However, its implications take many years to fully understand. This can only be accomplished through observing quality Staffordshires over the years and reading as much about the breed as possible. Many books have been written about the breed, and it is well worth the Staffordshire owner's time and effort to digest their contents if he or she is interested in showing or breeding this dog.

There are some breeds that change drastically from puppyhood to adulthood. It is extremely difficult for the untrained eye to determine the actual breed of some purebred dogs in puppyhood. This is not quite so with the Staffordshire. Most are inclined to agree that in many respects, a six-week-old Staffordshire puppy will reflect in miniature what he will look like at maturity.

It must be remembered, however, that the breed standard describes the "perfect" Staffordshire, but no dog is perfect and no Staffordshire, not even the greatest dog show winner, will possess every quality asked for in its perfect form. It is how closely an individual dog adheres to the standard for the breed that determines his show potential.

Above all, a Staffordshire should convey an appearance of strength and vigor. One without the other makes the Staffordshire useless, lacking in breed type. The Staffordshire standard asks for a dog that is sound in both body and temperament.

Although the standard takes great pains to describe in detail what is desirable in the breed, in the end, the reader should come away with the picture of a dog that owns the ground he stands upon; sound of both limb and mind; never too small, or too big. He is a medium-sized dog, and the opposite ends of the size spectrum do not conjure up a dog that is at once both strong and vigorous.

The look of the Staffordshire both in body and expression underscores his character—kind, courageous, and dignified. That is the essence of the Staffordshire temperament.

Proportion, balance, and symmetry are the keynote in assessing Staffordshire quality. The parts "fit." A head that is too large or a body that is too small would never give the total picture of what the standard conveys. Look at the dog in profile. The line of the balanced dog seems to flow from the tip of the Staffordshire's chin to the end of his tail.

Above all else, the Staffordshire Bull Terrier should convey the appearance of strength and vigor, appearing sound in both body and temperament.

THE OFFICIAL STANDARD OF THE STAFFORDSHIRE BULL TERRIER

General Appearance– The Staffordshire Bull Terrier is a smooth-coated dog. It

should be of great strength for its size and, although muscular, should be active and agile.

Size, Proportion, Substance–Height at shoulder: 14 to 16 inches. Weight: Dogs, 28 to 38 pounds; bitches, 24 to 34 pounds, these heights being related to weights. Nonconformity with these limits is a fault. In proportion, the length of back, from withers to tail set, is equal to the distance from withers to ground.

Head–Short, deep through, broad skull, very pronounced cheek muscles, distinct stop, short foreface, black nose. Pink (Dudley) nose to be considered a serious fault. **Eyes**–Dark preferable, but may bear some relation to coat color. Round, of medium size, and set to look straight ahead. Light eyes or pink eye rims to be considered a fault, except that where the coat surrounding the eye is white the eye rim may be pink. **Ears**–Rose or half-pricked and not large. Full drop or full prick to be considered a serious fault. **Mouth**–A bite in which the outer side of the lower incisors touches the inner side of the upper incisors.

The Staffordshire Bull Terrier's legs are straight and well boned, and his coat is smooth and close to the skin.

The lips should be tight and clean. The badly undershot or overshot bite is a serious fault.

Neck, Topline, Body–The neck is muscular, rather short, clean in outline and gradually widening toward the shoulders. The body is close coupled, with a level topline, wide front, deep brisket and well sprung ribs being rather light in the loins. The tail is undocked, of medium length, low set, tapering to a point and carried rather low. It should not curl much and may be likened to an old-fashioned pump handle. A tail that is too long or badly curled is a fault.

Forequarters–Legs straight and well boned, set rather far apart, without looseness at the shoulders and showing no weakness at the pasterns, from which point the feet turn out a little. Dewclaws on the forelegs may be removed. The feet should be well padded, strong and of medium size.

Hindquarters—The hindquarters should be well muscled, hocks let down with stifles well bent. Legs should be parallel when viewed from behind. Dewclaws, if any, on the hind legs are generally removed. Feet as in front.

Although he is a muscular dog, the Staffordshire should also be athletic and active. Ch. Guardstock Red Atom, the first Staffordshire to win an all-breed Best in Show in the US.

Coat—Smooth, short and close to the skin, not to be trimmed or de-whiskered.

Color—Red, fawn, white, black or blue, or any of these colors with white. Any shade of brindle or any shade of brindle with white. Black-and-tan or liver color to be disqualified.

Gait—Free, powerful and agile with economy of effort. Legs moving parallel when viewed from front or rear. Discernible drive from hind legs.

Temperament—From the past history of the Staffordshire Bull Terrier, the modern dog draws its character of indomitable courage, high intelligence, and tenacity. This, coupled with its affection for its friends, and children in particular, its off-duty quietness and trustworthy stability, makes it a foremost all-purpose dog.

Disqualification
Black-and-tan or liver color.
Approved November 14, 1989
Effective January 1, 1990

SELECTING the Right Staffordshire for You

The Staffordshire puppy you bring into your home will be your best friend and a member of your family for many years to come. The average well-bred and well-cared-for Staffordshire can lead a happy, active life for 10, 12, or even 15 years. Early care and sound breeding are vital to the longevity of your Staffordshire. Therefore, it is of the utmost importance that the dog you select has had every opportunity to begin life in a healthy, stable environment and comes from stock that is both physically and temperamentally sound.

The only way you can be assured of this is to go directly to a breeder of Staffordshires who has consistently produced dogs of this kind over the years. A breeder earns this reputation through a well-planned breeding program that has been governed by rigid selectivity. Selective breeding programs are aimed at maintaining the breed's many fine qualities and keeping the breed free of as many genetic weaknesses as possible.

Anyone who has ever bred dogs will quickly tell you that this selective process is both time-consuming and costly for a breeder, and that no one ever makes money breeding sound and healthy dogs. One of the many things it does accomplish, however, is to ensure that you get a Staffordshire that will be a joy to own. Responsible Staffordshire breeders protect their tremendous investment of time and money by basing their breeding programs on the healthiest, most representative breeding stock available. These breeders provide each following generation with the very best care, sanitation, and nutrition available.

Governing kennel clubs in the different countries of the world maintain lists of local breed clubs and breeders that can lead a prospective Staffordshire buyer to responsible breeders of quality stock. If you are not sure of where to contact an established Staffordshire breeder in your area, we strongly recommend contacting your local or governing kennel club for recommendations.

Occasionally, some pet shops offer Staffordshire puppies for sale. It should be understood that the pet shop owner seldom has any real knowledge of the puppy's background or what kind of care he received in the critical period from birth until the time he arrived in the shop.

You may be able to find an established Staffordshire breeder in your own area. Finding a local breeder will allow you to visit the breeder's home or kennel, inspect the facility, and, in many cases, see a puppy's parents and other relatives. Good breeders are always willing and able to discuss any problems that might exist in the breed and how they should be dealt with.

If there aren't any Staffordshire breeders in your immediate area, rest assured that taking the time and exerting the effort to plan a trip to visit a reputable breeder will be well worth your while. Shipping Staffordshires by air, whether they are puppies or adults, is a risky business at best, and many Staffordshire breeders simply will not do so.

Never hesitate to ask the breeder you visit or speak to on the phone any questions or concerns you might have relative to Staffordshire ownership. Expect any Stafford breeder you contact to ask many questions of you as well. Good breeders are just as interested in placing their Staffordshire puppies in a loving and safe environment as you are in

How do you choose just one? Finding a quality Staffordshire Bull Terrier begins with finding a reputable breeder.

obtaining a happy, healthy puppy.

Very few good breeders maintain large kennels these days, as it has become cost prohibitive. Actually, you are more apt to find Staffordshires that come from the homes of small hobby breeders who keep a few dogs and have litters only occasionally. Hobby breeders are equally dedicated to breeding quality Staffordshires. A factor in favor of the hobby breeder is his distinct advantage of being able to raise his puppies in the home environment, with all the accompanying personal attention and socialization.

Again, it is important that both the buyer and the seller ask questions. Be extremely suspicious of anyone who is willing to sell you a Staffordshire puppy with no questions asked.

Responsible breeders will screen all of their Staffordshires for genetic problems before breeding in order to produce the best puppies possible.

RECOGNIZING A HEALTHY PUPPY

Staffordshire breeders seldom release their puppies until they are at least eight weeks of age and have been given all of their puppy inoculations. By the time the litter is eight weeks of age, the puppies are entirely weaned and no longer nursing. While puppies are nursing, they have complete immunity from their mother. Once they have stopped nursing, however, they become highly susceptible to many infectious diseases. A number of these diseases can be transmitted to the hands and clothing of humans. Therefore, it is extremely important that your puppy is current on all the shots he must have for his age.

A healthy Staffordshire puppy is a bouncy, playful extrovert—never phlegmatic! His attitude should be happy and friendly. Personalities and temperaments within a litter can range from very active to somewhat passive. Some puppies are ready to play with the world, and others simply want to crawl

When visiting a breeder, make sure that the puppies are clean, healthy-looking, and well taken care of.

up into your lap and be held. Although you must never select a puppy that appears shy or listless because you feel sorry for him, do not hesitate to select the puppy that is a bit more quiet and reserved–that personality may suit yours just fine.

The important thing is that the puppy is healthy. Taking a puppy that appears sickly and needy will undoubtedly lead to heartache and expensive veterinary costs. Do not attempt to make up for what the breeder did not do in providing proper care and nutrition. It seldom works.

If you select one of the very active puppies, you must be sure that you have the extreme patience that will be needed to train him. This type of puppy might be very intelligent but demanding and contrary. Like a precocious child, this type of Staffordshire likes to have his own way. You must be prepared to meet this very challenging personality with patience, firmness, love, and consistency. We cannot stress the word *consistency* enough!

Pick the puppy that picks you. The Staffordshire you are considering should be interested in you and curious about the world around him.

Ask the breeder if it is at all possible to take the Stafford puppy you are attracted to into a different room in the kennel or house in which he was raised. The smells will remain the same for the puppy, so he should still feel secure, but it will give you an opportunity to see how the puppy acts away from his littermates and to inspect the puppy more closely.

Above all, the puppy should be clean. The coat should be shiny and soft to the touch. The insides of a healthy puppy's ears will be pink and clean. Dark discharge from the ears or a bad odor could indicate ear mites, a sure sign of lack of cleanliness and poor maintenance. A Staffordshire puppy's breath should always smell sweet. The nose of a healthy puppy is cold and wet, and there should be no discharge of any kind. There should never be any malformation of the jaw, lips, or nostrils and make sure there is no rupture of the navel.

The puppy's teeth must be clean, white, and bright, and the eyes should be dark and clear. Runny eyes or eyes that appear red and irritated could be caused by a myriad of problems, none of which indicate a healthy puppy. Coughing or diarrhea are absolute danger signals.

While Staffordshire puppies cannot be accused of being the epitome of style and grace, their movement still should be free and easy, and they should never express any difficulty in moving about. Sound conformation can be determined even at eight or ten weeks of age.

The puppy's attitude tells you a great deal about his state of health. Puppies that are feeling "out of sorts" react very quickly and will usually find a warm littermate to snuggle up to and prefer to stay that way even when the rest of the gang wants to play or go exploring.

MALE OR FEMALE

The sex of a dog in many breeds is an important consideration, and of course there are sex-related differences in the Staffordshire that the prospective buyer should consider. In the end, however, the assets and liabilities of each sex do balance each other out and the final choice remains one of individual preference.

The male Staffordshire simply has more of everything—more size, more weight, more aggressiveness (particularly around other males!), and more to care for. So often we hear that a female makes the best companion. This is not particularly so. A male Staffordshire makes just as loving, devoted, and trainable a companion as the female. He can be a bit more headstrong as an adolescent and require a bit more patience on the part of his owner. Again, the owner's dedication to establishing and maintaining discipline will determine the final outcome.

Female Staffords are often more tolerant of other dogs than their brothers. Their maternal instincts give them a bit more sense of family. Females do have their semi-annual heat cycles once they have reached sexual maturity. These cycles usually occur for the first time at about nine or ten months of age and are accompanied by a bloody vaginal discharge. The discharge creates a need to confine the female so that she does not soil her surroundings. It must be understood that the female has no control over this bloody discharge, so it has nothing to do with training. Confinement of the female in heat is also especially important to prevent unwanted attention from some neighborhood Lothario.

The sexually related problems of both the female and male can be eliminated by neutering the pet Staffordshire (spaying the female and castrating the male). Unless a Stafford is purchased expressly for breeding or showing from a breeder capable of making this judgment, your pet should be sexually altered.

It should be understood, however, that spaying and neutering are not reversible procedures. Spayed females or neutered males are not allowed to be shown in the conformation shows of most countries, nor will altered animals ever be able to be used for breeding.

BREEDING

Breeding and raising Staffordshire Bull Terriers should be left in the hands of people who have the facilities and knowledge to do the job properly. Only those who have the facilities to keep each and every puppy they breed until the correct home is found for him should ever contemplate raising a litter. This can often take many months after a litter is born. After all, Staffords do not appear on the top-ten popularity poll, and strangers will not be knocking down your door for puppies. Most single-dog owners are not equipped to hold an entire litter of puppies until each and every one of the pups finds an ideal owner.

Breeding should only be attempted by people who have the time and the means to care for the mother and the resulting puppies.

Naturally, a responsible dog owner would never allow his or her pet to roam the streets and end his life in an animal shelter. Unfortunately, being forced to place a puppy due to space constraints before you are able to thoroughly check out the prospective buyer may in fact create this exact situation.

Parents will often ask to buy a female just as a pet but with intentions of breeding so that their children can witness "the miracle of birth." There are countless books and videos now available that portray this wonderful event. Sexually altering one's companion dogs eliminates bothersome household problems and precautions and promotes good health and responsible dog ownership.

SELECTING A SHOW-PROSPECT PUPPY

If you are considering a show career for your puppy, we strongly advise putting yourself in the hands of an established breeder who has earned a reputation for breeding winning show dogs. They are most capable of anticipating what one might expect a young puppy of their line to develop into when he reaches maturity.

Although the potential buyer should read the official standard of perfection for the Staffordshire, it is hard for the novice to really understand the nuances of what is being asked for. The experienced breeder is best equipped to do so and will be only too happy to assist you in your quest. Even at that, no one can make accurate predictions or guarantees about a very young puppy.

Any predictions a breeder is apt to make are based upon the breeder's experience with past litters that produced winning show dogs. It should be obvious that the more successful a breeder has been in producing winning Staffordshires through the years, the broader his or her basis of comparison will be.

The most any responsible breeder will say about an eight-week-old puppy is that he has "show potential." If you are serious about showing your Staffordshire, most breeders strongly suggest waiting until a puppy is at least four or five months old before making any decisions.

There are many beauty-point shortcomings that a Staffordshire puppy might have that would in no way interfere with his being a wonderful companion. At the same time, these faults could be serious drawbacks in the showring. Many of these faults are such that a beginner in the breed might hardly notice. This is why employing the assistance of a good breeder is so important. Still, the prospective buyer should be at least generally aware of what the Staffordshire show puppy should look like and know which faults are considered serious as far as the breed standard is concerned. The Staffordshire Bull Terrier standard lists only one disqualification and that is for color. Staffords that are black-and-tan or liver colored may not be shown at American Kennel Club (AKC) shows.

The AKC also has disqualifications that it has set for all breeds as well. Sexually altered dogs of either sex and males missing one or both testicles may not be shown at AKC conformation events. Dogs that attack people or other dogs are also subject to temporary or permanent disqualification.

All of the previously described characteristics of a sound and healthy companion puppy apply to the show puppy as well. The show prospect must be sound, healthy, and adhere to the standard of the breed very closely.

The complete AKC standard for the Staffordshire appears in this book, and there are also a number of other books that can assist the newcomer in furthering their knowledge of the Stafford. The more you know about the history and development of the breed, the better equipped you will be to see the differences that distinguish the show dog from the pet.

The characteristics that really define a show-prospect puppy are type, balance, and temperament. These three simple words have so many nuances that it takes most breeders an entire lifetime to fully comprehend even a part of what they convey.

A little puppy is a big responsibility, so be sure that you have carefully considered dog ownership before taking a Staffordshire Bull Terrier puppy home.

Type

Type includes the characteristics that truly set a breed apart. All dogs

There are certain characteristics that your Staffordshire must possess to be a success in the show ring.

have four legs and are expected to use them efficiently, but there are certain characteristics that make a Stafford distinct and recognizable from all other breeds. These characteristics are included in the standard for the breed, and most breeders feel very strongly that a show-prospect puppy should possess as many of these important and distinguishing characteristics as possible.

Balance

Balance is the manner in which all the desirable characteristics fit together. The balanced dog's parts just seem to flow easily from one to the next. Their combination and transition creates a picture of quality that says, "I am the best Staffordshire Bull Terrier that ever was!"

Temperament

The correct Staffordshire temperament combines all those wonderful characteristics that we have been discussing. In the show ring, the Staffordshire is a solid performer that makes it obvious that he owns every inch of the ground he stands on.

Whether you choose an adult or puppy, the Staffordshire Bull Terrier can make a wonderful and affectionate companion.

PUPPY OR ADULT

For the person anticipating a show career for their Stafford or for someone hoping to become a breeder, the purchase of a young adult provides greater certainty of quality. Even those who simply want a companion could consider the adult dog.

In some instances, breeders will have males or females that they no longer wish to use for breeding, and after the dogs have been altered, they would prefer to have them live out their lives in a private home with all its attendant care and attention. Acquiring an adult dog eliminates the many problems that raising a puppy involves, and Staffordshires are a breed that can "transfer" well, provided they are given the affection and attention they need.

Elderly people often prefer the adult dog, particularly one that is housebroken. The adult dog can be easier to manage, requiring less supervision and damage control. Adult Staffords are seldom chewers and are usually more than ready to adapt to household rules.

There are things to consider, though. Adult dogs have usually developed behaviors that may or may not fit into your routine. If an adult Staffordshire has never been exposed to small children, the dog may be totally perplexed by this new experience. However, never, under any condition, should the dog snap or be aggressive. Any Stafford that attempts to bite should be euthanized.

The breeder will have started your Staffordshire puppy on the road to good nutrition, so stick to this original diet and make any changes gradually.

Then, too, there is the problem of other pets. A Staffordshire that has never been around other animals, particularly cats, will probably have an extremely difficult, if not impossible, task of adjusting to them.

We strongly advise taking an adult Staffordshire on a trial basis to see if the dog will adapt to the new owner's lifestyle and environment. Most often it works out, but on rare occasions, a prospective owner decides training his or her dog from puppyhood is worth the time and effort required.

IMPORTANT PAPERS

The purchase of any purebred dog entitles you to four very important documents: a health record, which includes a list of inoculations, a copy of the dog's pedigree, the registration certificate, and a health guarantee.

Health and Inoculation Records

You will find that most Staffordshire breeders have initiated the necessary preliminary inoculation series for their puppies by the time they are eight weeks of age. These inoculations

Socialization with littermates is very important in order to teach your Staffordshire to get along with other dogs when he matures.

temporarily protect the puppies against hepatitis, leptospirosis, distemper, and canine parvovirus. Permanent inoculations will follow at a prescribed time. Because breeders and veterinarians follow different approaches to inoculations, it is important that the health record you obtain for your puppy accurately lists which shots have been given and when. In this way, the veterinarian you choose will be able to continue on with the appropriate inoculation series as needed. In most cases, rabies inoculations are not given until a puppy is six months of age or older.

Pedigree

The pedigree is your dog's family tree. The breeder must supply you with a copy of this document authenticating your puppy's ancestors back to at least the third generation.

All purebred dogs have pedigrees. The pedigree in itself does not mean that your puppy is of show quality. All it means is that all of his ancestors were, in fact, registered Staffordshires. They may all have been of pet quality.

Unscrupulous puppy dealers often try to imply that a dog with a pedigree indicates that he is of championship caliber. This is not true. Again, it simply tells you that all of the dog's ancestors are purebred.

Registration Certificate

A registration certificate is the canine world's birth certificate. This certificate is issued by a country's governing kennel club. When the ownership of your Staffordshire is transferred from the breeder's name to your name, the transaction is entered on this certificate, and once mailed to the appropriate kennel club, it is permanently recorded in their computerized files.

Keep all of your dog's documents in a safe place, as you will need them when you visit your veterinarian or if you ever wish to breed or show your Staffordshire. Keep the name, address, and phone number of the breeder from whom you purchase your dog in a separate place as well. If you ever lose

For the first few weeks of life, puppies get the nutrients they need from nursing. After that, they rely on the breeder to provide them with the proper nutrition.

Happy and healthy Staffordshire puppies are a reflection of their breeder's good care.

any of these important documents, you will then be able to contact the breeder regarding obtaining duplicates.

Health Guarantee

Any reputable breeder is more than willing to supply a written agreement that the purchase of your Staffordshire is contingent upon his passing a veterinarian's examination. Ideally, you will be able to arrange an appointment with your chosen veterinarian right after you have picked up your puppy from the breeder and before you take the puppy home. If this is not possible, you should not delay this procedure any longer than 24 hours from the time you take your puppy home.

DIET SHEET

Your Staffordshire is the happy, healthy puppy he is because the breeder has been carefully feeding and caring for him. Every breeder we know has their own particular way of doing this. Most breeders give the new owner a written record that

details the amount and brand of food that a puppy has been receiving. Follow these recommendations to the letter, at least for the first month or two after the puppy comes to live with you.

The diet sheet should indicate the kinds of food and number of times a day your puppy has been accustomed to being fed. The kind of vitamin supplementation, if any, the puppy has been receiving is also important. Following the breeder's prescribed procedure will reduce the chance of upset stomach and loose stools.

Usually, a breeder's diet sheet projects the increases and changes in food that will be necessary as your puppy grows from week to week. If the sheet does not include this information, ask the breeder for suggestions regarding increases and the eventual changeover to adult food.

In the unlikely event you are not supplied with a diet sheet by the breeder and are unable to get one, your veterinarian will be able to advise you in this respect. There are countless foods now being manufactured expressly to meet the nutritional needs of puppies and growing dogs. A trip down the pet aisle of your supermarket will prove just how many choices there are. Two important tips to remember: Read labels carefully for content and when dealing with established, reliable manufacturers, you are more likely to get what you pay for.

TEMPERAMENT AND SOCIALIZATION

Temperament is shaped by both heredity and environment. Inherited good temperament can be ruined by poor treatment and lack of proper socialization. A Staffordshire puppy that comes from shy or nervous stock or stock that is uncontrollably aggressive is a risk, either as a companion or show dog and has no place in the home or in a breeding program. Therefore, it is critical that you obtain a happy puppy from a breeder who is determined to produce good temperaments and has taken all the necessary steps to provide the early socialization necessary.

Bring your puppy with you wherever you go—the more people your Staffordshire Bull Terrier meets, the better socialized he will become.

Taking your puppy to puppy kindergarten class is one of the best things you can do for him. There he will learn

Each puppy is an individual and should be treated as one. Spending time with different people and in different situations will allow your Staffordshire to develop confidence.

basic household manners, as well as how to interact with other dogs and people. He absolutely must learn to walk on a leash at your side without pulling, and he needs to learn this as a puppy.

Temperaments in the same litter can range from confident and outgoing on the high end of the scale to quiet and contemplative at the other end, but, by and large, the Staffordshire temperament is and should be confident and friendly.

If you are fortunate enough to have children in the household or living nearby, your socialization task will be assisted considerably. Staffordshires raised with well-supervised children are the best. The two seem to understand each other and, in some way known only to the puppies and children themselves, they give each other the confidence to face the trying ordeal of growing up.

The children in your own household are not the only children your puppy should spend time with. It is a case of the more the merrier! Every child (and adult for that matter) that enters your household should be introduced to your Staffordshire. If trustworthy children live nearby, have them come in and spend time with your puppy if there is adult supervision. The children must understand, however, that they should never overexert your puppy by playing too roughly or for too long a time.

A puppy that is going to compete in conformation shows must become accustomed to being handled by judges

Weather permitting, your puppy should go everywhere with you: the post office, the market, the shopping mall— wherever. Be prepared to create a stir wherever you go. Everyone loves puppies and will want to pet your little fellow. There is nothing in the world better for a puppy.

When doing your errands, however, never leave your dog alone in the car during weather in which the temperatures can be considered warm. Temperatures in a closed car rise to surprising and life-threatening heights in minutes. Nor can Stafford owners consider leaving their dog alone in a car with the windows open. The theft rate and escape rate among Staffords is alarmingly high.

The young Staffordshire will quickly learn that all humans— young and old, short and tall, and of all races—are friends. You are in charge. You must call the shots.

If your Staffordshire has a show career in his future, there are other things that will have to be taught in addition to just being handled. All Staffordshire show dogs must learn to have their mouth inspected by the judge. The judge must also be able to check the teeth. Males must be accustomed to having their testicles touched, as the dog show judge must determine that all male dogs are complete, which means that there are two normal-sized testicles in the scrotum. These inspections must begin in puppyhood and be done on a regular and continuing basis.

THE ADOLESCENT STAFFORDSHIRE

Staffordshires mature very slowly. While some breeds are mature at 12 months and most others at 24 months, the Staffordshire is fast approaching 3 years of age before most consider him finished with all those stages. Some lines, however, may achieve maturity a bit earlier.

Staffordshires go through growth periods in spurts. Parts of the anatomy seem to develop independently of each other, so that a Staffordshire puppy may look one way today and still another the following week. The little tank may take on the look of a space rocket practically overnight. Despair not, eventually your puppy will undoubtedly revert back to what he gave promise of at eight weeks of age.

Food needs change during this growth period. Think of Staffordshire puppies as individualistic as children and act accordingly. The amount of food that you give your growing Staffordshire should be adjusted to how much the dog will consume at each meal and how that amount relates to optimum weight. Most Staffordshires are good eaters, and you must be extremely careful not to let them get too fat.

Some Staffordshires will give you that forlorn look that says that they are at starvation's doorstep, regardless of how much food you give them. Excess weight for Staffordshires can be lethal. If the entire meal is eaten quickly, add a small amount to the next feeding and continue to do so as the need increases. This method will ensure that you give your puppy enough food, but you must also pay close attention to your Staffordshire's appearance.

At eight weeks of age, a Staffordshire puppy is eating four meals a day. By the time he is six months old, the puppy can do well on two meals a day, with perhaps a snack in the middle of the day. If your puppy does not eat the food offered, he is either not hungry or not well. Your dog will eat when he is hungry. If you suspect the dog is not well, a trip to the veterinarian is in order.

This adolescent period is a particularly important one, because it is the time your Staffordshire must learn all the household and social rules by which he will live for the rest of his life. Your patience and commitment during this time will not only produce a respected canine good citizen but will forge a bond between the two of you that will grow and ripen into a wonderful relationship.

HEALTH CONCERNS

In nature, genetically transferred infirmities that would interfere with an animal's ability to nurse, to capture food as an adult, or to escape from a predator would automatically eliminate the individual from the gene pool. Controlled breeding of domesticated dogs dictates saving all the puppies in a litter for both humanitarian and financial reasons. However, in preserving life we also perpetuate health problems. Thus, our humanitarian proclivities have a downside as well.

Before you purchase a Staffordshire puppy, make sure you have educated yourself about the medical problems that can affect the breed.

Like all breeds of domesticated dog, the Stafford has its share of hereditary problems; fortunately, the problems are relatively few. The diseases described here will rarely be present in the Stafford you buy from a respected breeder, nor will these problems necessarily be found in your Stafford's immediate ancestors. They are breed problems, however, that should be discussed with the breeder from whom you purchase your dog. As stated previously, the reputable Stafford breeder is aware of the following problems and should be more than willing to discuss them with you.

51

Breathing Problems

The brachycephalic (short-headed) breeds can be prone to breathing problems due to the foreshortening of the breathing apparatus. The restrictions can range from minor and unnoticeable to extreme respiratory distress. Some of these problems can be surgically corrected. It should be understood that when these corrective measures are taken, the dog becomes ineligible to be shown at AKC shows.

Juvenile Cataracts

Normally speaking, cataracts are a condition associated with older dogs; however, it is not entirely uncommon to find cataracts among the young in some breeds of dog. Some Stafford puppies are affected. Diagnosis and treatment must be conducted by an eye specialist.

Responsible breeders have the parents of their litters certified as being free of eye abnormalities. The Canine Eye Registry Foundation (CERF) issues the certificates, and testing must be redone annually. It is important to ask to see these certificates before buying a dog.

Congenital Epilepsy

Epilepsy is a short lasting but extreme disturbance of the nerve activity of the brain. The seizures are recurrent, unprovoked, and unpredictable. In Staffords, it can occur at three to five years of age. Epilepsy can be clinically diagnosed and kept under control with medication.

Patella Luxation

This condition is also commonly referred to as "slipping stifles." It is an abnormality of the stifle or knee joint leading to dislocation of the kneecap (patella). Normally, the kneecap is held in position by strong and elastic ligaments. If the ligament is loose or the groove is insufficiently developed, the kneecap will leave its normal position and slip to one side or the other of the track in which it is normally held. The dog may exhibit an intermittent but persistent limp or have difficulty straightening out the knee. Treatment may require surgery.

Hip Dysplasia (HD)

This is a developmental disease of the hip joint. The normal

All Staffordshire Bull Terriers should be screened for genetic defects before breeding in order to ensure healthy offspring and preserve the quality of the breed.

hip is best described as a ball-and-socket arrangement. The upper bone of the rear leg (the femur) has a head that should fit neatly and firmly into the socket of the pelvis. Proper construction allows the femur to rotate freely while being held firmly within the socket. In the case of hip dysplasia, the socket is shallow, allowing the femur head to slip and slide. The shallower the socket, the more dislocation and the more it can impair movement and cause pain.

The only way of knowing whether or not a dog is free of hip dysplasia is through an Orthopedic Foundation for Animals (OFA) or PennHip™ screening. A dog must be 24 months old before a final determination can be made; therefore, it is critical that you ask to see the OFA clearances on the sire and dam of the puppy you are considering.

CARING for Your Staffordshire Bull Terrier

FEEDING AND NUTRITION

The best way to make sure your Staffordshire puppy is obtaining the right amount and the correct type of food for his age is to follow the diet sheet provided by the breeder from whom you obtain your puppy. If you do your best not to change the puppy's diet, you will be less apt to run into digestive problems and diarrhea. Diarrhea is very serious in young puppies. Puppies with diarrhea can dehydrate very rapidly, causing severe problems and even death.

If it is necessary to change your Staffordshire puppy's diet for any reason, it should be done gradually, over a period of several meals and a few days. Begin by adding a few tablespoons of the new food, gradually increasing the amount until the meal consists entirely of the new product.

By the time your Staffordshire is 10 to 12 months old, you can reduce feedings to one or at the most two a day. The main meal can be given either

For the best diet for your Staffordshire Bull Terrier puppy, consult your breeder or veterinarian.

Make sure you choose a good-quality dog food that is appropriate for your Staffordshire's stage of life and activity level. Puppies will need a growth formula.

in the morning or evening. It is really a matter of choice on your part. There are two important things to remember: Feed the main meal to your dog at the same time every day and make sure what you feed him is nutritionally complete.

The single meal can be supplemented by a morning or nighttime snack of hard dog biscuits made especially for large dogs. These biscuits not only become highly anticipated treats, but are genuinely helpful in maintaining healthy gums and teeth.

Balanced Diets

In order for a canine diet to qualify as complete and balanced in the United States, it must meet standards set by the Subcommittee on Canine Nutrition of the National Research Council of the National Academy of Sciences. Most commercial foods manufactured for dogs prove that they meet these standards by listing the ingredients contained in the food on every package or can. The ingredients are listed in descending order, with the main ingredient listed first.

Fed with any regularity at all, refined sugars can quickly cause your Staffordshire to become obese and will definitely create tooth decay. Candy stores do not exist in nature, and canine teeth are not genetically disposed to handling sugars. Do not feed your Staffordshire candy or sweets and avoid products that contain sugar to any high degree.

All a healthy Staffordshire needs to be offered are fresh water and a properly prepared, balanced diet containing the essential nutrients in correct proportions. Dog foods come canned, dry, semi-moist, "scientifically fortified," and "all-natural." A visit to your local supermarket or pet store will reveal the vast array from which you will be able to select.

Putting your Staffordshire on a regular feeding schedule will help you monitor how much your dog is eating. This puppy looks like he's getting some help finishing his meals.

Wild carnivores eat the entire beast they capture and kill. The carnivore's kills consist almost entirely of herbivores (plant-eating) animals, and invariably the carnivore begins its meal with the contents of the herbivore's stomach. This provides the carbohydrates, minerals, and nutrients present in vegetables.

Through centuries of domestication, we have made our dogs entirely dependent upon us for their well-being. Therefore, we are entirely responsible for duplicating the food balance that the wild dog finds in nature. The domesticated dog's diet must include some protein, carbohydrates, fats, roughage, and small amounts of essential minerals and vitamins.

Finding commercially prepared diets that contain all the necessary nutrients in the proper balance will not present a problem. It is important to understand, though, that these commercially prepared foods do contain most of the nutrients your Staffordshire requires. Most Staffordshire breeders

There may be times in your Staffordshire's life that he will need supplements, but only give him what is prescribed by your veterinarian.

recommend vitamin supplementation for a healthy coat and increased stamina, especially for show dogs, pregnant bitches, or growing puppies.

Oversupplementation

A great deal of controversy exists today regarding the orthopedic problems that afflict many breeds. Some claim these problems are entirely hereditary conditions, but many others feel they can be exacerbated by overuse of mineral and vitamin supplements for puppies. Oversupplementation is now looked upon by some breeders as a major contributor to many skeletal abnormalities found in the purebred dogs of today. In giving vitamin supplementation, you should never exceed the prescribed amount. No vitamin, however, is a substitute for a nutritious, balanced diet.

Pregnant and lactating bitches do require supplementation of some kind, but again, less is more, and it should always be given erring on the side of moderation. Extreme caution is advised in this case, and the situation is best discussed with your veterinarian.

Make sure your Staffordshire Bull Terrier has plenty of cool clean water available, especially when exercising outside.

If the owner of a Staffordshire normally eats healthy, nutritious food, there is no reason why their dog cannot be given some table scraps. What could possibly be harmful in good, nutritious food?

Table scraps should be given only as part of the dog's meal and never from the table. A Staffordshire that becomes accustomed to being handfed from the table can quickly become a real pest at mealtime. Also, dinner guests may find the pleading stare and vocalization of your Staffordshire less than appealing when dinner is being served.

Dogs do not care if food looks like a hot dog or a piece of cheese. Truly nutritious dog foods are seldom manufactured to look like food that appeals to humans. Dogs only care about how food smells and tastes. It is highly doubtful that you will be eating your dog's food, so do not waste your money on products that look fit for human consumption.

Special Diets

There are curently a number of commercially prepared diets for dogs with special dietary needs. The overweight, underweight, or geriatric dog can have his nutritional needs met, as can puppies and growing dogs. The calorie content of these foods is adjusted accordingly. With the correct amount of the right foods and the proper amount of exercise, your Staffordshire should stay in top shape. Again, common sense must prevail. Too many calories will increase weight; too few will reduce weight.

Occasionally, a young Staffordshire that is going through the teething period will become a poor eater. The concerned owner's first response is to tempt the dog by handfeeding him special treats and foods that the problem eater seems to prefer. This practice only serves to compound the problem. Once the dog learns to play the waiting game, he will turn up his nose at anything other than his favorite food, knowing full well what he wants to eat will eventually arrive.

Unlike humans, dogs have no suicidal tendencies. A healthy dog will not starve himself to death. He may not eat enough to keep himself in the shape that we find ideal and attractive, but he will definitely eat enough to maintain himself. If your Staffordshire is not eating properly and appears to be too thin, it is probably best to consult your veterinarian.

SPECIAL NEEDS OF THE STAFFORDSHIRE BULL TERRIER

Heat and Your Staffordshire

Like all purebred dogs, Staffordshires are a man-made breed, but man has fashioned this breed in such a way that it requires very special care in hot weather. Anyone who wants a Staffordshire must clearly understand these needs and be willing to accept responsibility

Pregnant Staffordshires need extra care and a special diet. Make sure you consult your veterinarian about your Staf's diet at this time.

Staffordshire Bull Terriers are affected by hot weather, so limit your dog's exercise and outdoor time when temperatures are high.

for whatever measures must be taken to ensure their execution.

Our hard and fast rule regarding Staffordshires and heat is that there should be no exertion or playing when temperatures are up and humidity is high. If a Staffordshire begins to pant, steps must be taken immediately to cool the dog down.

Travel

Heat problems encountered while traveling can be minimized by air-conditioned cars. However, if this is not possible, a cooler filled with ice and towels will help considerably. The cold towels can be placed at the bottom of your Stafford's travel crate and exchanged as they lose their effectiveness.

Never stop in hot weather until you get where you are going, especially if you have to turn off the air conditioning in your car. Once you arrive, get your Staffordshire into air-conditioned quarters without too long a delay. An extreme change from cool to hot can be particularly devastating.

Never leave your dog in situation where he cannot get out of direct sunlight. If you are forced to keep your Staffordshire in the sun in hot weather for a brief period, put a wet towel over the dog's body and head and keep him off asphalt or concrete.

If there is no air conditioning at your destination, gradually increase the temperature in your car so that you will not have to take your Staffordshire from a cold vehicle into high heat. This is too much of a shock, and the dog will start panting immediately. Needless to say, you must never leave your Staffordshire alone in an automobile. Even on overcast days, temperatures can soar in just minutes.

While you might consider taking your Staffordshire along on your summer vacation, think about the situation carefully. It will take a great deal of prior planning and may restrict your freedom considerably. Your Staffordshire is much better off staying home where he can be carefully supervised.

If air travel is on your Staffordshire's schedule, discuss this with your veterinarian. He or she might advise tranquilizing your dog to preclude stress. Oxygen deprivation during flights is a serious threat to your Staffordshire. Furthermore, most baggage attendants have no idea how dangerous it is to allow your Staffordshire's shipping container to sit on the tarmac in the summer sun.

No matter how many dogs you may have owned in the past, when it comes to Staffordshires and heat—the situation is entirely different!

Exercise

With everything said about Staffordshires' reaction to heat, it may sound as if they should never be allowed outside of an air-conditioned room. This is not so. Proper exercise in the cool of the morning or evening is as vital to the Staffordshire's longevity as is proper nutrition.

The Staffordshire is not a breed that requires taking your energy level to its outer limits, but if the proper time of day is chosen, your Stafford can pretty much keep up with the average jogger or power walker. Moderated steady exercise that keeps your companion's heart rate in the low working area will do nothing but extend his life. If your Staffordshire is doing all this with you at his side, you are increasing the chances that the two of you will enjoy each other's company for many more years to come.

Toys and Chewing

Even as puppies, Staffordshires have great jaw strength for their size and can be very destructive during their teething period. It is said that a Staffordshire puppy is part private investigator and part vacuum cleaner. They find things that have yet to be lost and feel everything they find should be filed in their tummies.

Puppy proofing your home is a must. Your Staffordshire will be ingenious in getting into things he shouldn't, so you have to be far more clever and keep ahead of what your puppy might get himself into.

Provide toys that will keep the puppy busy and eliminate his need for eating your needlepoint pillow or the legs of your Chippendale table. Just be sure to provide things that are hard to chew up such as the original Nylabone™, and never give him anything gummy or soft. Rawhide, no matter what size and shape when new, eventually flattens out and can become lodged in the

Provide your Staffordshire puppy with plenty of safe chew toys to keep his jaws exercised and his teeth healthy.

Puppies need to chew in order to develop both physically and mentally. Chewing on toys will save your furniture from puppy teeth marks.

throat, as can beef jerky or hot dogs. You should not give a Staffordshire meat bones unless they are the huge beef knuckle bones, and even those are risky. Staffordshires can chew up almost anything and may get a perforated or compacted intestine.

You will want to have a large bottle of liquid Bitter Apple and some of the Bitter Apple furniture paste to put on things that you do not want your Staffordshire to chew on. The product can be purchased at both pharmacies and hardware stores. Most dogs loathe the taste of this product, but it is not harmful to the dog.

Staffordshires love shoes of all types and will often grab at the very shoes you are wearing as you are walking along. This is hazardous to both you and your dog. Never give your puppy old shoes to play with. Dogs can see no difference between an old sneaker you have given them and your brand new dress shoes. Once you've worn the shoes, they all smell exactly alike to your Staffordshire—age and cost notwithstanding!

Puppies possess a lot of energy, but they also need a lot of rest. This Staf puppy looks flat-out exhausted.

Socialization

The Staffordshire is by nature a happy dog and takes most situations in stride, but it is important to accommodate the breed's natural instincts by making sure he is accustomed to everyday events of all kinds. Traffic, strange noises, loud or hyperactive children, and strange animals can be very intimidating to a dog of any breed that has never experienced them before. Gently and gradually introduce your puppy to as many strange situations as you possibly can.

Illness and Injury

One problem with nearly all the bull-and-terrier crosses is that their threshold of pain is extremely high. This seems as if it would be a real plus, but it most definitely is not. Because it takes some Staffords so long to show visible signs of discomfort or symptoms, by the time you realize he is ill or sustained an internal injury, a dog could be in the critical stage. For this reason, we strongly recommend having a veterinarian that understands this situation.

BATHING AND GROOMING

The Stafford does not have a long coat to contend with, but that does not mean the breed needs no grooming. Regular attendance to this matter assists both your Stafford's health and his appearance. Your puppy should become accustomed to standing quietly on a grooming table for his weekly "once-over." A stiff-bristle brush applied with the lay of the hair will whisk away what little debris the Stafford's coat holds, and a soft towel will restore the coat's shine.

Brushing should always be done in the same direction as the hair grows. You should begin at the dog's head, brushing toward the tail and down the sides and legs. This procedure will loosen the dead hair and brush it off the dog. This is also the time to check the skin thoroughly for any abrasions or external parasites.

Nail Trimming

Staffordshires that do not get enough exercise on rough surfaces to wear their nails down must have them clipped or filed down on a regular basis. While grooming, accustom your dog to having his feet inspected. Always inspect your dog's feet for cracked pads. Pay particular attention to any swollen or tender areas. Check between the toes for splinters and thorns.

The nails of a Staffordshire can grow long very quickly. Do not allow the nails to become overgrown and then expect to cut them back easily. Each nail has a blood vessel running through the center called the quick. The quick grows close to the end of the nail and contains very sensitive nerve endings. If the nail is allowed to grow too long, it will be impossible to cut it back to a proper length without cutting into the quick. This causes severe pain to the dog and can also result in a great deal of bleeding that can be very difficult to stop.

Nails can be trimmed with canine nail clippers, an electric nail grinder (also called a drummel), or a coarse file made expressly for that purpose. All three of these items can be purchased at major pet emporiums.

We prefer the electric nail grinder above the others,

If you accustom your dog to grooming procedures like nail clipping at an early age, he will become used to the process as he matures.

because it is so easy to control and helps avoid cutting into the quick. Dark nails make it practically impossible to see where the quick ends. Regardless of which nail-trimming device is used, one must proceed with caution and remove only a small portion of the nail at a time.

The use of the electric grinder requires introducing your puppy to it at an early age. The instrument makes a whining sound, not unlike a dentist's drill. The noise combined with the vibration of the sanding head on the nail itself can take some getting used to, but most dogs we have used it on eventually accept it as one of life's trials. Most Staffordshires do not like having their nails trimmed no matter which device is used, so our own eventual decision was to use the grinder, because we were less apt to damage the quick.

If the quick is nipped in the trimming process, there are a number of blood-clotting products available at pet shops that will almost immediately stem the flow of blood. It is wise to have one

Regular brushing can help keep your Staffordshire Bull Terrier's coat shiny and healthy-looking.

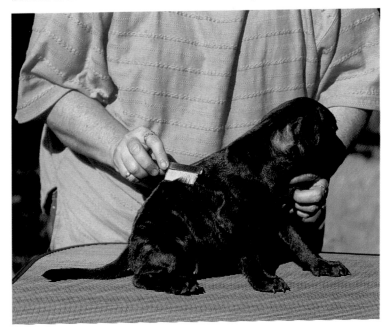

If you groom your Staffordshire on a daily basis, he will seldom need a bath. This Staffordshire doesn't seem to mind bath time at all.

of these products on hand in case there is a nail-trimming accident or the dog tears a nail on his own.

If brushing is attended to regularly, bathing will seldom be necessary, unless your Staffordshire finds his way into something that leaves his coat with a disagreeable odor. Even then, there are many products, both dry and liquid, available at your local pet store that eliminate odors and leave the coat shiny and clean.

A damp washcloth will help you put the Staffordshire that has given himself a mud bath back in shape very quickly. However, if your Staffordshire's coat becomes wet in cold weather, be sure to towel down the dog thoroughly. The Staffordshire is a thin-coated dog that can catch a chill easily.

Check the skin inside the thighs and armpits to see if it is dry or red. Artificial heat during winter months can dry out the skin and cause it to become chapped. Place a small amount of petroleum jelly or baby oil on the palms of your hands and rub your hands over the dry areas. Staffordshires are also subject to dry noses. In extreme cases, the nose leather can shrivel and crack. Avoid this by regular applications of petroleum jelly.

HOUSEBREAKING and Training Your Staffordshire

There is no breed of dog that cannot be trained; however, some breeds appear to be more difficult to get the desired response from than others. This is more apt to be due to the trainer not being "Staffordshire specific" in his or her approach to the training than the dog's inability to learn.

Training ease depends in great part on just how much a dog depends upon his master's approval. The entirely dependent dog lives to please his master and will do everything in his power to evoke the approval response from the person he is devoted to. At the opposite end of the pole, we have the totally independent dog that is not remotely concerned with what his master thinks. Dependency varies from one breed to the next and within breeds as well. Staffordshires are no exception to this rule. Successfully training a Staffordshire depends upon your fully understanding the breed's character and dealing with it accordingly. No one should even think about attempting to train a Stafford unless they are prepared to lend a firm hand and commanding voice.

Some professionals who train dogs advise obtaining a puppy on the 49th day of his life. Their research indicates that it is at this precise point in time that a puppy is most ready to bond to a human and subsequently depend upon that person for approval. Prior to that time, the puppy needs to be with his siblings and mother. Just after the 49th day, the puppy passes through varying stages that make him less equipped for human bonding and more independent in nature.

We are sure that not all behaviorists will ascribe to the 49th day theory, but there does seem to be general agreement that the optimum time to bring a puppy into his new home is at about seven to eight weeks of age. It is wise to at least consider this information and discuss it with the breeder from whom you will be purchasing your puppy.

At first, it may appear cute and funny when your puppy bites your hands or feet, refuses to give up a toy, or jumps on you. However, allowing your puppy to do this encourages the behavior, and the dog will continue to do this into adulthood, which will be far from cute and funny and extremely difficult to stop.

The problem with battles of will is that the Staffordshire's history of tenacity is then evoked and the dog becomes an immovable object. When this immovable object (the Staffordshire) meets the irresistible force (his owner), well, little more need be said!

This is not to say that there are no rules or regulations in Staffordshire training. On the contrary, it is very important when training a Staffordshire that the dog be absolutely confident of his place in the pack, *The majority of* which is the human or humans that the *Staffordshire Bull* dog lives with. The Staffordshire's *Terriers live in* place in the pecking order must be *households and must* below every family member, and this *learn to obey the* must be clear to the dog from the first *rules of the family.* day he enters his new home.

HOUSEBREAKING

Without a doubt, the best way to housebreak a Staffordshire is to use the crate method. First-time dog owners are initially inclined to see the crate or cage method of housebreaking as cruel, but those same people will return later and thank me profusely for having suggested it in the first place. All dogs need a place of their own to retreat to, and you will find that the Staffordshire will consider his crate his den or place of refuge.

The use of a crate reduces housetraining time down to an absolute minimum and avoids keeping a puppy under constant stress by incessantly correcting him for making mistakes in the house. The anti-crate advocates consider it cruel to confine a puppy for any length of time, but find no problem in constantly harassing and punishing the puppy because he has wet on the carpet or relieved himself behind the sofa.

Make sure your Staffordshire puppy has plenty of time outside to attend to his needs.

The crate that you use for housebreaking should only be large enough for the puppy to stand up, lie down, and stretch out in comfortably. These cages are available at most pet emporiums at a wide range of prices. It is not necessary to dash out and buy a new crate every few weeks to accommodate the Staffordshire's rapid spurts of growth. Simply cut a piece of plywood sized to partition off the excess space in the very large cage and move it back as needed.

Begin feeding your puppy in the crate. Keep the door closed and latched while the puppy is eating. When the meal is finished, open the cage and carry the puppy outdoors to the spot where you want him to learn to eliminate. As you are doing so, you should consistently use the same words. Whether the words are "go out," "potty," or whatever else you feel comfortable saying, it makes no difference. The important point is that the puppy will be learning both where to

Crate training is the easiest way to housebreak your Staffordshire puppy, because dogs do not like to soil where they eat and sleep.

eliminate and that certain words mean something is expected of him.

In the event that you do not have outdoor access or will be away from home for long periods of time, begin housebreaking by placing newspapers in some out of the way corner that is easily accessible to the puppy. If you consistently take your puppy to the same spot, you will reinforce the habit of going there for that purpose.

Do not let the puppy loose after eating. Young puppies will eliminate almost immediately after eating or drinking. They will also be ready to relieve themselves when they first wake up and after playing. If you keep a watchful eye on your puppy, you will quickly learn when this is about to take place. A puppy usually circles and sniffs the floor just before he will relieve himself. Do not give your puppy an opportunity to learn that he can eliminate in the house! Your housetraining chores will be reduced considerably if you avoid allowing bad habits to begin in the first place.

If you are not able to watch your puppy every minute, he should be in his crate with the door securely latched. Each time you put your puppy in the crate, give him a small treat of some kind. Throw the treat to the back of the cage and encourage the puppy to walk in on his own. When he does so, praise the puppy and perhaps hand him another piece of the treat through the wires of the crate.

Do not succumb to your puppy's complaints about being in his crate. The puppy must learn to stay in his crate and to do so without unnecessary complaining. A quick no command and a tap on the crate will usually get the puppy to understand theatrics will not result in liberation.

Understand that a puppy of 8 to 12 weeks of age will not be able to contain himself for long

Puppies will have to eliminate after sleeping, eating, drinking, and playing. Take your puppy out immediately to avoid accidents in the house.

74

Keeping your puppy safely confined can help keep your Staffordshire, your house, and your yard safe.

periods of time. Puppies of that age must relieve themselves every few hours, except at night. Your schedule must be adjusted accordingly. Also, make sure your puppy has relieved himself, both bowel and bladder, the last thing at night, and do not dawdle when you wake up in the morning.

Your first priority in the morning is to get the puppy outdoors. Just how early this ritual will take place will depend much more on your puppy than on you. If your Staffordshire is like most other puppies, there will be no doubt in your mind when he needs to be let out. You will also very quickly learn to tell the difference between the "this-is-an-emergency" complaint and the "I-just-want-out" grumbling. Do not test the young puppy's ability to contain himself. His vocal demand to be let out is confirmation that the housebreaking lesson is being learned.

If you find it necessary to be away from home all day, you will not be able to leave your puppy in a crate, but on the other hand, do not make the mistake of allowing him to roam the house or even a large room at will. Confine the puppy to a small room or partitioned-off area and cover the floor with newspaper. Make this area large enough so that the puppy will not have to relieve himself next to his bed or his food or water bowls. You will soon find that the puppy will be inclined to use one particular spot to perform his bowel and bladder functions. When you are home, you must take the puppy to this exact spot to eliminate at the appropriate time.

Your puppy must get used to wearing a collar and leash, not only for his safety but for the safety of others.

BASIC TRAINING

Early puppy kindergarten, along with puppy play training, is vital if you plan to do obedience work of any kind. The human trainer has to be absolutely dedicated, have a good sense of humor, and have lots of patience.

How you are feeling emotionally and the environment in which you train are just as important to your dog's training as his state of mind is at the time. Never begin training when you are irritated, distressed, or preoccupied, nor should you begin basic training in a place that interferes with your or your dog's concentration. Once the commands are understood and learned, you can begin testing your dog in public places, but at first the two of you should work in a place where you can concentrate fully upon each other.

The No Command

There is no doubt whatsoever that one of the most important commands your Staffordshire puppy will ever learn is the meaning of the no command. It is critical that the puppy learns this command just as soon as possible. One important

Once your Staffordshire is accustomed to his collar and leash, you can begin to take him on walks around the neighborhood.

piece of advice in using this and all other commands—never give a command you are not prepared and able to follow through on. The only way a puppy learns to obey commands is to realize that once issued, commands must be complied with. Learning the no command should start on the first day of the puppy's arrival at your home.

Leash Training

It is never too early to accustom the Staffordshire puppy to a collar and leash. It is your way of keeping your dog under control. Although it may not be necessary for the puppy or adult Staffordshire to wear his collar and identification tags within the confines of your home, no Staffordshire should ever leave home without a collar and without the leash held securely in your hand.

Begin getting your Staffordshire puppy accustomed to his collar by leaving it on for a few minutes at a time. Gradually extend the time you leave the collar on. Most Staffordshires become accustomed to their collar very quickly and forget they are even wearing one.

Once this is accomplished, attach a lightweight leash to the collar while you are playing with the puppy. Do not try to guide him at first. The point is to accustom the puppy to the feeling of having something attached to the collar.

Some Staffordshire puppies adapt to their collar very quickly, and without any undo resistance, learn to be guided with the leash. Other Staffordshire puppies may be absolutely adamant that they will not have any part of leash training and seem intent on strangling themselves before submitting.

If your puppy is one of the latter, do not continue to force the issue. Simply create a lasso with your leash and put your Staffordshire's head and front legs through the lasso opening so that the leash encircles the puppy's shoulders and chest, just behind the front legs. Some puppies seem to object to this method less than having the leash around their neck.

If that doesn't work either, consider using a harness. Most pet emporiums carry special harnesses, and dog specialty houses can order harnesses especially created for the bull-and-terrier breeds.

At any rate, encourage your puppy to follow you as you move away. If the puppy is reluctant to cooperate, coax him along with a treat of some kind. Hold the treat in front of the puppy's nose to encourage him to follow you. Just as soon as the puppy takes a few steps toward you, praise him enthusiastically and continue to do so as you move along.

Teaching your Staffordshire to walk on a leash will make your daily outings much more enjoyable.

The sit command is the foundation for all the other commands your Staffordshire Bull Terrier will learn.

Make the initial sessions very brief and enjoyable. Continue the lessons in your home or yard until the puppy is completely unconcerned about the fact that he is on a leash. With a treat in one hand and the leash in the other, you can begin to use both to guide the puppy in the direction you wish to go. Your walks can begin in front of the house and eventually extend down the street and around the block. This is one lesson no puppy is too young to learn.

The Come Command

The next most important lesson for the Staffordshire puppy to learn is to come when called; therefore, it is very important that the puppy learn his name as soon as possible. When teaching a puppy his name, constant repetition does the trick. Use the name every time you talk to your puppy.

Learning to come on command could save your Staffordshire's life when the two of you venture out into the world. Come is the command that a dog must understand has to be obeyed without question, but the dog should not associate that command with fear. Your dog's response to his name and the word "come" should always be associated with a pleasant experience, such as great praise and petting, or particularly in the case of the Staffordshire, a food treat.

In Staffordshire training, it is far easier to avoid the establishment of bad habits than it is to correct them once set. Never give the come command unless you are sure your Staffordshire puppy will come to you. The very young puppy is far more inclined to respond to learning the come command than the older Staffordshire. Initially, use the command when the puppy is already on his way to you or give the command while walking or running away from the youngster. Clap your hands and sound very happy and excited about having the puppy join in on this game.

Treats, along with plenty of praise and attention, can be great training motivators for your Staffordshire puppy.

The very young Staffordshire will normally want to stay as close to his owner as possible, especially in strange surroundings. When your puppy sees you moving away, his natural inclination will be to get close to you. This is a perfect time to use the come command.

Later, as the puppy grows more independent and more headstrong (as you now know a Staffordshire can do), you may want to attach a long leash or rope to the puppy's collar to ensure the correct response. Do not chase or punish your puppy for not obeying the come command. Doing so in the initial stages of training makes the youngster associate the command with unpleasant consequences, which will result in avoidance rather than the immediate positive response you desire. It is imperative that you praise your Staffordshire puppy and give him a treat when he does come to you, even if he voluntarily delays responding for many minutes.

The Sit and Stay Commands

Just as important to your Staffordshire's safety (and your sanity!) as the no command and learning to come when called are the sit and stay commands. Even very young Staffordshires can learn the sit command quickly, especially if it appears to be a game and a food treat is involved.

The sit command helps to teach your puppy self-control. For puppies, sitting still is the hardest part.

First, remember that the Staffordshire-in-training should always be on a collar and leash for all his lessons. A Staffordshire is certainly not beyond getting up and walking away when he has decided enough is enough!

In training most dogs, the trainer would give the sit command immediately before pushing down on the dog's hindquarters. Pushing down on the rear quarters does not work well with Staffordshires. They have a strong tendency to resist any force.

A much better way to help your dog sit is to take your left hand or forearm (depending upon the size of the dog) and place it across the back legs at the hocks. Then place your hand on the dog's chest. Holding the back legs, gently push the dog back by applying pressure to the chest until the dog sits. Praise the dog lavishly when he does sit, even though it is you who made the action take place. Again, a food treat held over the head and moved back always seems to get the lesson across to the learning Staffordshire.

Hand signals used in conjunction with verbal commands can be very effective when training your Staffordshire Bull Terrier. This Staf obeys the stay signal.

Put your hand lightly on the dog's rear and repeat the sit command several times. If your dog makes an attempt to get up, repeat the command yet again while exerting pressure on the chest. Make your Staffordshire stay in this position for increasing lengths of time. Begin with a few seconds and increase the time as lessons progress over the following weeks.

If your Staffordshire student attempts to get up or to lie down, he should be corrected by simply saying, "Sit!" in a firm voice. This should be accompanied by returning the dog to the desired position.

Once your Staffordshire has begun to understand the sit command, you may be able to assume the position by simply putting your hand on the dog's chest and exerting slight backward pressure. All of this should be done as gently as possible. It can really be next to impossible to push a Staffordshire's rear end down without exerting so much pressure that you could conceivably cause an injury to the dog's hips or stifle joints.

Your dog should only get up when you decide that he is allowed to do so. Do not test the young Staffordshire's patience to the limits. Remember that you are dealing with a baby, and the attention span of any youngster is relatively short.

When you do decide the dog can get up, call his name, say "OK," and make a big fuss over him. Praise and a food treat are in order every time your Staffordshire responds correctly.

Once your Staffordshire has mastered the sit lesson you may start on the stay command. With your Staffordshire on leash and facing you, command him to sit, then take a step or two back. If your dog attempts to get up to follow, firmly say, "Sit, stay!" While you are saying this, raise your hand, palm toward the dog, and again command, "Stay!"

Any attempt on your dog's part to get up must be corrected at once, returning him to the sit position and repeating, "Stay!" Once your dog begins to understand what you want, you can gradually increase the distance you step back. With a long leash attached to your dog's collar (even a clothesline will do), start with a few steps and gradually increase the distance to several yards. Your Staffordshire must eventually learn that the sit/stay command must be obeyed no matter how far away you are. Later on, with advanced training, your dog will learn that the command is to be obeyed even when you move entirely out of sight.

When you first begin to release him from the command, avoid calling the dog to you. This makes the dog overly anxious to get up and run to you. Until your Staffordshire masters the sit lesson and is able to remain in the sit position for as long as you dictate, walk back to your dog and say, "OK," which is a signal that the command is over. Later, when your dog becomes more reliable in this respect, you can call him to you.

The sit/stay lesson can take considerable time and patience, especially with a Staffordshire puppy whose attention span will be very short. It is best to keep the stay part of the lesson to a minimum until the Staffordshire is at least five or six months old. Everything in a very young Staffordshire's makeup will urge him to follow you wherever you go. Forcing a very young Staffordshire to operate against his natural instincts can be bewildering for the puppy.

The Down Command

Once your Staffordshire has mastered the sit and stay commands, you may begin work on the down command. This is the single-word command for lie down. Use the down command only when you want the dog to lie down. If you want your Staffordshire to get off your sofa or to stop jumping up on people, use the off command. Do not interchange these two commands. Doing so will only serve to confuse your dog and evoking the right response will become next to impossible.

The down position is especially useful if you want your Staffordshire to remain in a particular place for a long period of time. A Staffordshire is far more inclined to stay put when he is lying down than when he is sitting.

Because it represents submission, the down command may be difficult for your Staffordshire to master.

Teaching this command to your Staffordshire may take more time and patience than the previous lessons

that the two of you have undertaken. It is believed by some animal behaviorists that assuming the down position somehow represents submissiveness to the dog. Considering the self-willed nature of our Staffordshires, it is easy to understand how this command could prove more difficult for them to comply with. In the end, once the down command has become a part of the Staffordshire's repertory, it seems to be more relaxing for the dog and you will find that he seems less inclined to get up and wander off.

With your Staffordshire sitting in front of and facing you, hold a treat in your right hand with the excess part of the leash in your left hand. Hold the treat under the dog's nose and slowly bring your hand down to the ground. Your dog will follow the treat with his head and neck. As he does, give the command, "Down."

An alternative method of getting your Staffordshire headed into the down position is to move around to the dog's right side and as you draw his attention downward with your right hand, slide your left arm under the dog's front legs and gently slide them forward. In the case of a small puppy, you will undoubtedly have to be on your knees next to the youngster.

As your Staffordshire's forelegs begin to slide out to his front, keep moving the treat along the ground until the dog's whole body is lying on the ground, while you continually repeat, "Down." Once your dog has assumed the position you desire, give him the treat and a lot of praise. Continue assisting your Staffordshire into the down position until he does so on his own. Be firm and be patient.

The Heel Command

In learning to heel, your Staffordshire will walk on your left side with his shoulder next to your leg, no matter which direction you might go or how quickly you turn. Teaching your Staffordshire to heel will not only make your daily walks far more enjoyable, it will make him a far more tractable companion when the two of you are in crowded or confusing situations.

A Staffordshire usually wants to be with you wherever you go, so training him to walk along in the correct position is usually not much of a problem. A link-chain training collar is very useful for the heeling lesson for most Staffords. It provides both quick pressure around the neck and a snapping sound, both of which get the dog's attention. Erroneously referred to as a choke collar, the link-chain collar, when used properly, will not choke the dog.

There are some Staffords that are extremely sensitive about what is put around their necks, so in this case, a flat buckle collar is best. The pet shop at which you purchase your supplies can be most helpful in advising you about which collar might be best for your dog. If you are using a harness, it may take a bit more time to get the heel message across to your Stafford. Persevere and you'll both get there with patience.

As you train your Staffordshire puppy to walk along on the leash, you should accustom the youngster to walk on your left side. The leash should cross your body from the dog's collar to your right hand. The excess portion of the leash will be folded into your right hand and your left hand will be used to make corrections with the leash.

When learning to heel, your Staffordshire should walk on your left side with his shoulder next to your leg, no matter which direction you go.

A quick, short jerk on the leash with your left hand will keep your Staffordshire from lunging side to side, pulling ahead, or lagging back. As you make a correction, give the heel command. Always keep the leash slack, as long as your dog maintains the proper position at your side.

If your dog begins to drift away, give the leash a sharp jerk, guide the dog back to the correct position, and give the "heel" command. Do not pull on the lead with steady pressure. You must be very careful of a Staffordshire's throat. What is needed is a sharp but gentle jerking motion to get your Staffordshire's attention. Remember, it is always a jerk and release motion.

TRAINING CLASSES

There are actually few limits to what a patient, consistent

The versatile and eager-to-please Staffordshire can be trained to compete in any event. Dolly, owned by Elinda Anderson, sails over the bar jump in an agility competition. Staffordshire owner (and the accent is most definitely on patient and consistent!) can teach his or her dog. Once the lesson is mastered, your Staffordshire will perform with enthusiasm and gusto, especially if he has learned that all of these "'silly" things that you have taught him to do will result in a lot of fun and praise.

Don't forget that you are dealing with a breed that has that good old Bulldog tenacity in his blood. It may take a bit of time to get through, but once you do, be aware that the Staffordshire is one of the most intelligent and wonderful breeds of dog known to man. Your Staffordshire performs because he has decided he wants to, not because you are forcing him to obey. Do not tell your Staffordshire this, but if you are persistent enough in your training, your Staffordshire will eventually think the whole thing was his own idea in the first place!

For advanced obedience work beyond the basics, it is wise for the Staffordshire owner to consider local professional assistance. Professional trainers have had long-standing experience in avoiding the pitfalls of obedience training and can help you to avoid them as well.

This training assistance can be obtained in many ways. The unfamiliar dogs and new people encountered at training classes are particularly good for your Staffordshire's socialization. There are free-of-charge classes at many public parks and recreation facilities, as well as very formal and sometimes very expensive individual lessons with private trainers.

There are also some obedience schools that will take your Staffordshire and train him for you. However, unless your schedule provides no time at all to train your own dog, having someone else train the dog for you would be last on my list of recommendations. The rapport that develops between the owner who has trained his or her Staffordshire to be a pleasant companion and good canine citizen is very special—well worth the time and patience it requires.

Training your Staffordshire Bull Terrier for the Canine Good Citizen® will make him a welcome addition to your family.

VERSATILITY

Once your Staffordshire has been taught his basic manners, there are countless ways that the two of you can participate in enjoyable events. The breed is highly successful in conformation shows and has proven it can also do well in obedience competition.

There are Canine Good Citizen certificates that can be earned through the American Kennel Club. Staffordshires have also proven to be wonderful therapy dogs, which visit homes for the aged, orphanages, and hospitals. Staffordshires love people, and people are always interested in the dogs because of their looks. It is amazing to see how kind and gentle some otherwise comical and rowdy Staffordshires will behave with people who are ill or feeble or with small children. It has been proven these visits provide great therapeutic value to patients.

The well-trained Staffordshire can provide a whole world of activities for his owner. You are only limited by the amount of time you wish to invest in this remarkable breed.

SPORT of Purebred Dogs

**W**elcome to the exciting and sometimes frustrating sport of dogs. No doubt you are trying to learn more about dogs or you wouldn't be deep into this book. This section covers the basics that may entice you, further your knowledge, and help you to understand the dog world.

Dog showing has been a very popular sport for a long time and has been taken quite seriously by some. Others only enjoy it as a hobby.

The Kennel Club in England was formed in 1859, the American Kennel Club was established in 1884, and the Canadian Kennel Club was formed in 1888. The purpose of these clubs was to register purebred dogs and maintain their Stud Books. In the beginning, the concept of registering dogs was not readily accepted. More than 36 million dogs have been enrolled in the AKC Stud Book since its inception in 1888. Presently the kennel clubs not only register dogs but adopt and enforce rules and regulations governing dog shows, obedience trials, and field trials. Over the years they have fostered and encouraged interest in the health and welfare of the purebred dog. They routinely donate funds to veterinary research for study on genetic disorders.

Below are the addresses of the kennel clubs in the United States, Great Britain, and Canada.

The American Kennel Club
260 Madison Avenue
New York, NY 10016
(Their registry is located at: 5580 Centerview Drive, STE 200, Raleigh, NC 27606-3390)

The Kennel Club
1 Clarges Street
Piccadilly, London, WIY 8AB, England

The Canadian Kennel Club
100-89 Skyway Avenue
Etobicoke, Ontario M6S 4V7
Canada

Today there are numerous activities that are enjoyable for both the dog and the handler. Some of the activities include conformation showing, obedience competition, tracking, agility, the Canine Good Citizen Certificate, and a wide range of instinct tests that vary from breed to breed. Where you start depends upon your goals, which early on may not be readily apparent.

PUPPY KINDERGARTEN

Every puppy will benefit from this class. PKT is the foundation for all future dog activities from conformation to "couch potatoes." Pet owners should make an effort to attend even if they never expect to show their dog. The class is designed for puppies about three months of age with graduation at approximately five months of age. All the puppies will be in the same age group and, even though some may be a little unruly, there should not be any real problem. This class will teach the

Puppy kindergarten is a great place to learn basic obedience, as well as a good way to socialize your Staffordshire with other dogs.

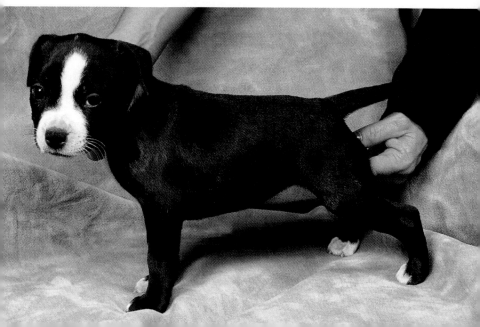

Even if you never enter a dog show, every puppy and owner can benefit from the bond that is formed through basic training.

puppy some beginning obedience. As in all obedience classes the owner learns how to train his own dog. The PKT class gives the puppy the opportunity to interact with other puppies in the same age group and exposes him to strangers, which is very important. Some dogs grow up with behavior problems, one of them being fear of strangers. As you can see, there can be much to gain from this class.

There are some basic obedience exercises that every dog should learn. Some of these can be started with puppy kindergarten.

CONFORMATION

Conformation showing is our oldest dog show sport. This type of showing is based on the dog's appearance—that is his structure, movement, and attitude. When considering this type of showing, you need to be aware of your breed's standard and be able to evaluate your dog compared to that standard. The breeder of your puppy or other experienced breeders would be good sources for such an evaluation. Puppies can go through lots of changes over a period of time. Many puppies start out as promising hopefuls and then after maturing may be disappointing as show candidates. Even so this should not deter them from being excellent pets.

In conformation, your Staffordshire Bull Terrier will be judged on how closely he conforms to the standard of the breed.

Usually conformation training classes are offered by the local kennel or obedience clubs. These are excellent places for training puppies. The puppy should be able to walk on a lead before entering such a class. Proper ring procedure and technique for posing (stacking) the dog will be demonstrated as well as gaiting the dog. Usually certain patterns are used in the ring such as the triangle or the "L." Conformation class, like the PKT class, will give your youngster the opportunity to socialize with different breeds of dogs and humans, too.

It takes some time to learn the routine of conformation showing. Usually one starts at the puppy matches that may be AKC Sanctioned or Fun Matches. These matches are generally for puppies from two or three months to a year old, and there may be classes for the adult over the age of 12 months. Similar to point shows, the classes are divided by sex and after

93

completion of the classes in that breed or variety, the class winners compete for Best of Breed or Variety. The winner goes on to compete in the Group and the Group winners compete for Best in Match. No championship points are awarded for match wins.

A few matches can be great training for puppies even though there is no intention to go on showing. Matches enable the puppy to meet new people and be handled by a stranger–the judge. It is also a change of environment, which broadens the horizon for both dog and handler. Matches and other dog activities boost the confidence of the handler and especially the younger handlers.

Earning an AKC championship is built on a point system, which is different from Great Britain. To become an AKC Champion of Record the dog must earn 15 points. The number of points earned each time depends upon the number of dogs in competition. The number of points available at each show depends upon the breed, its sex, and the location of the show. The United States is divided into ten AKC zones. Each zone has its own set of points. The purpose of the zones is to try to equalize the points available from breed to breed and area to area.The AKC adjusts the point scale annually.

The number of points that can be won at a show are between one and five. Three-, four-, and five-point wins are considered majors. Not only does the dog need 15 points won under three different judges, but those points must include two majors under two different judges. Canada also works on a point system but majors are not required.

Dogs always show before bitches. The classes available to those seeking points are: Puppy (which may be divided into 6 to 9 months and 9 to 12 months); 12 to 18 months; Novice; Bred-by-Exhibitor; American-bred; and Open. The class winners of the same sex of each breed or variety compete against each other for Winners Dog and Winners Bitch. A Reserve Winners Dog and Reserve Winners Bitch are also awarded but do not carry any points unless the Winners win is disallowed by AKC. The Winners Dog and Bitch compete with the specials (those dogs that have attained championship) for Best of Breed or Variety, Best of Winners, and Best of Opposite Sex. It is possible to pick up an extra point or even a major if the points are higher for the defeated winner than those of

Best of Winners. The latter would get the higher total from the defeated winner.

At an all-breed show, each Best of Breed or Variety winner will go on to his respective Group and then the Group winners will compete against each other for Best in Show. There are seven Groups: Sporting, Hounds, Working, Terriers, Toys, Non-Sporting, and Herding. Obviously there are no Groups at specialty shows (those shows that have only one breed or a show such as the American Spaniel Club's Flushing Spaniel Show, which is for all flushing spaniel breeds).

Handlers should wear comfortable clothes that do not distract from the appearance of their dog and allow them to move freely about the ring.

Earning a championship in England is somewhat different since they do not have a point system. Challenge Certificates are awarded if the judge feels the dog is deserving regardless of the number of dogs in competition. A dog must earn three Challenge Certificates under three different judges, with at least one of these Certificates being won after the age of 12 months. Competition is very strong and entries may be higher than they are in the US. The Kennel Club's Challenge Certificates are only available at Championship Shows.

In England, The Kennel Club regulations require that certain dogs, Border Collies and Gundog breeds, qualify in a working capacity (i.e., obedience or field trials) before becoming a full Champion. If they do not qualify in the working aspect, then they are designated a Show Champion, which is equivalent to the AKC's Champion of Record. A Gundog may be granted the title of Field Trial Champion (FT Ch.) if he passes all the tests in the field but would also have to qualify in conformation before becoming a full Champion. A Border Collie that earns the title of Obedience Champion (Ob Ch.) must also qualify in the conformation ring before becoming a Champion.

The US doesn't have a designation full Champion but does award for Dual and Triple Champions. The Dual Champion must be a Champion of Record, and either Champion Tracker, Herding Champion, Obedience Trial Champion, or Field Champion. Any dog that has been awarded the titles of Champion of Record, and any two of the following: Champion Tracker, Herding Champion, Obedience Trial Champion or Field Champion, may be designated as a Triple Champion.

Owners of Staffordshires must be willing to invest time in training their dog in order to give him a productive outlet for his intelligence and energy.

The shows in England seem to put more emphasis on breeder judges than those in the US. There is much competition within the breeds. Therefore, the quality of the individual breeds should be very good. In the United States we tend to have more "all around judges" (those that judge multiple breeds) and use the breeder judges at the specialty shows. Breeder judges are more familiar with their own breed because they are actively breeding that breed or did so at one time. Americans emphasize Group and Best in Show wins and promote them accordingly.

The shows in England can be very large and extend over several days, with the Groups being scheduled on different days. Though multi-day shows are not common in the US, there are cluster shows, where several different clubs will use the same show site over consecutive days.

Westminster Kennel Club is our most prestigious show although the entry is limited to 2500. In recent years, entry has been limited to Champions. This show is more formal than the majority of the shows with the judges wearing formal attire and the handlers fashionably dressed. In most instances the quality of the dogs is superb. After all, it is a show of Champions. It is a good show to study the AKC registered breeds and is by far the most exciting–especially because it is televised! WKC is one of the few shows in this country that is still benched. This means the dog must be in his benched area during the show hours except when he is being groomed, in the ring, or being exercised.

Typically, the handlers are very particular about their appearances. They are careful not to wear something that will

detract from their dog but will perhaps enhance him. American ring procedure is quite formal compared to that of other countries. There is a certain etiquette expected between the judge and exhibitor and among the other exhibitors. Of course it is not always the case but the judge is supposed to be polite, not engaging in small talk or acknowledging how well he knows the handler. There is a more informal and relaxed atmosphere at the shows in other countries. For instance, the dress code is more casual. I can see where this might be more fun for the exhibitor and especially for the novice. The US is very handler-oriented in many of the breeds. It is true, in most instances, that the experienced professional handler can present the dog better and will have a feel for what a judge likes.

An exercise pen is just one of the many pieces of equipment you will need to bring with you to a dog show.

In England, Crufts is The Kennel Club's own show and is most assuredly the largest dog show in the world. They've been known to have an entry of nearly 20,000, and the show lasts four days. Entry is only gained by qualifying through winning in specified classes at another Championship Show. Westminster is strictly conformation, but Crufts exhibitors and spectators enjoy not only conformation but obedience, agility, and a multitude of exhibitions as well. Obedience was admitted in 1957 and agility in 1983.

If you are handling your own dog, please give some consideration to your apparel. For sure the dress code at matches is more informal than the point shows. However, you should wear something a little more appropriate than beach attire or ragged jeans and bare feet. If you check out the handlers and see what is presently fashionable, you'll catch on. Men usually dress with a shirt and tie and a nice sports coat. Whether you are male or female, you will want to wear comfortable clothes and shoes. You need to be able to run with your dog and you certainly don't want to take a chance of

Successful showing requires dedication and preparation, but most of all it should be enjoyable for both dog and handler.

falling and hurting yourself. Heaven forbid, if nothing else, you'll upset your dog. Women usually wear a dress or two-piece outfit, preferably with pockets to carry bait, comb, brush, etc. In this case men are the lucky ones with all their pockets. Ladies, think about where your dress will be if you need to kneel on the floor and also think about running. Does it allow freedom to do so?

You need to take along dog; crate; ex pen (if you use one); extra newspaper; water pail and water; all required grooming equipment, including hair dryer and extension cord; table; chair for you; bait for dog and lunch for you and friends; and, last but not least, clean up materials, such as plastic bags,

paper towels, and perhaps a bath towel and some shampoo—just in case. Don't forget your entry confirmation and directions to the show.

If you are showing in obedience, then you will want to wear pants. Many of our top obedience handlers wear pants that are color-coordinated with their dogs. The philosophy is that imperfections in the black dog will be less obvious next to your black pants.

Whether you are showing in conformation, Junior Showmanship, or obedience, you need to watch the clock and be sure you are not late. It is customary to pick up your conformation armband a few minutes before the start of the class. They will not wait for you and if you are on the show grounds and not in the ring, you will upset everyone. It's a little more complicated picking up your obedience armband if you show later in the class. If you have not picked up your armband and they get to your number, you may not be allowed to show. It's best to pick up your armband early, but then you may show earlier than expected if other handlers don't pick up. Customarily all conflicts should be discussed with the judge prior to the start of the class.

Junior Showmanship

The Junior Showmanship Class is a wonderful way to build self-confidence even if there are no aspirations of staying with the dog-show game later in life. Frequently, Junior Showmanship becomes the background of those who become successful exhibitors/handlers in the future. In some instances it is taken very seriously, and success is measured in terms of wins. The Junior Handler is judged solely on his ability and skill in presenting his dog. The dog's conformation is not to be considered by the judge. Even so the condition and grooming of the dog may be a reflection upon the handler.

In order to pass the Canine Good Citizen test, your Staffordshire must be able to get along with all kinds of people. This puppy looks like he has passed the test.

Usually the matches and point shows include different classes. The Junior Handler's dog may be entered in a breed or obedience class and even shown by another person in that class. Junior Showmanship classes are usually divided by age and perhaps sex.

The age is determined by the handler's age on the day of the show.

CANINE GOOD CITIZEN

The AKC sponsors a program to encourage dog owners to train their dogs. Local clubs perform the pass/fail tests, and dogs who pass are awarded a Canine Good Citizen Certificate. Proof of vaccination is required at the time of participation. The test includes:

1. Accepting a friendly stranger.
2. Sitting politely for petting.
3. Appearance and grooming.
4. Walking on a loose leash.
5. Walking through a crowd.
6. Sit and down on command/staying in place.
7. Come when called.
8. Reaction to another dog.
9. Reactions to distractions.
10. Supervised separation.

If more effort was made by pet owners to accomplish these exercises, fewer dogs would be cast off to the humane shelter.

OBEDIENCE

Obedience is necessary, without a doubt, but it can also become a wonderful hobby or even an obsession. Obedience classes and competition can provide wonderful companionship, not only with your dog but with your classmates or fellow competitors. It is always gratifying to discuss your dog's problems with others who have had similar experiences. The AKC acknowledged Obedience around 1936, and it has changed tremendously even though many of the exercises are basically the same. Today, obedience competition is just that–very competitive. Even so, it is possible for every obedience exhibitor to come home a winner (by earning qualifying scores) even though he/she may not earn a placement in the class.

Most of the obedience titles are awarded after earning three qualifying scores (legs) in the appropriate class under three different judges. These

Ch. Trumate Shadows Showcase, CGC, NA, or "Blazer," owned by Rachel Redsun, shows off his grace and athleticism.

classes offer a perfect score of 200, which is extremely rare. Each of the class exercises has its own point value. A leg is earned after receiving a score of at least 170 and at least 50 percent of the points available in each exercise. The titles are:

Companion Dog–CD
This is called the Novice Class and the exercises are:

1. Heel on leash and figure 8	40 points
2. Stand for examination	30 points
3. Heel free	40 points
4. Recall	30 points
5. Long sit–one minute	30 points
6. Long down–three minutes	30 points
Maximum total score	200 points

Companion Dog Excellent–CDX
This is the Open Class and the exercises are:

1. Heel off leash and figure 8	40 points
2. Drop on recall	30 points
3. Retrieve on flat	20 points
4. Retrieve over high jump	30 points
5. Broad jump	20 points
6. Long sit–three minutes (out of sight)	30 points
7. Long down–five minutes (out of sight)	30 points
Maximum total score	200 points

Utility Dog–UD

The Utility Class exercises are:

1. Signal Exercise	40 points
2. Scent discrimination-Article 1	30 points
3. Scent discrimination-Article 2	30 points
4. Directed retrieve	30 points
5. Moving stand and examination	30 points
6. Directed jumping	40 points
Maximum total score	200 points

After achieving the UD title, you may feel inclined to go after the UDX and/or OTCh. The UDX (Utility Dog Excellent) title went into effect in January 1994. It is not easily attained. The title requires qualifying simultaneously ten times in Open B and Utility B but not necessarily at consecutive shows.

Performance tests help dogs apply natural instincts, like using their noses, to the show ring.

The OTCh (Obedience Trial Champion) is awarded after the dog has earned his UD and then goes on to earn 100 championship points, a first place in Utility, a first place in Open, and another first place in either class. The placements must be won under three different judges at all-breed obedience trials. The points are determined by the number of dogs competing in the Open B and Utility B classes. The OTCh title precedes the dog's name.

Obedience matches (AKC Sanctioned, Fun, and Show and Go) are usually available. Usually they are sponsored by the local obedience clubs. When preparing an obedience dog for a title, you will find matches very helpful. Fun Matches and Show and Go Matches are more lenient in allowing you to make corrections in the ring. This type of training is usually very

Dolly, owned by Elinda Anderson, eagerly waits her turn in the ring at a bench show in Portland, Oregon.

necessary for the Open and Utility Classes. AKC Sanctioned Obedience Matches do not allow corrections in the ring because they must abide by the AKC Obedience Regulations. If you are interested in showing in obedience, then you should contact the AKC for a copy of the Obedience Regulations.

AGILITY

Agility was first introduced by John Varley in England at the Crufts Dog Show, February 1978, but Peter Meanwell, competitor and judge, actually developed the idea. It was officially recognized in the early '80s. Agility is extremely popular in England and Canada and growing in popularity in the US. The AKC acknowledged agility in August 1994. Dogs must be at least 12 months of age to be entered. It is a fascinating sport that the dog, handler, and spectators enjoy to the utmost. Agility is a spectator sport! The dog performs off lead. The handler either runs with his dog or positions himself on the course and directs his dog with verbal and hand signals over a timed course over or through a variety of obstacles including a time out or pause. One of the main drawbacks to agility is finding a place to train. The obstacles take up a lot of space and it is very time-consuming to put up and take down courses.

The titles earned at AKC agility trials are Novice Agility Dog (NAD), Open Agility Dog (OAD), Agility Dog Excellent (ADX), and Master Agility Excellent (MAX). In order to acquire an agility title, a dog must earn a qualifying score in his respective class on three separate occasions under two different judges. The MAX will be awarded after earning ten qualifying scores in the Agility Excellent Class.

Agility is a fast-paced sport that is enjoyable for both the dogs and the spectators. Dolly conquers the tire jump with ease.

Agility competitions test the Staffordshire Bull Terrier's coordination. Blazer heads to the next obstacle with enthusiasm.

PERFORMANCE TESTS

During the last decade the American Kennel Club has promoted performance tests–those events that test the different breeds' natural abilities. This type of event encourages a handler to devote even more time to his dog and retain the natural instincts of his breed heritage. It is an important part of the wonderful world of dogs.

Earthdog Events

Earthdog events are for small terriers (Australian, Bedlington, Border, Cairn, Dandie Dinmont, Fox (Smooth & Wire), Lakeland, Norfolk, Norwich, Scottish, Sealyham, Skye, Welsh, West Highland White and Dachshunds).

Limited registration (ILP) dogs are eligible and all entrants must be at least six months of age. The primary purpose of the small terriers and Dachshunds is to pursue quarry to ground, hold the game, and alert the hunter where to dig, or to bolt. There are two parts to the test: (1) the approach to the quarry and (2) working the quarry. The dog must pass both parts for a Junior Earthdog (JE). The Senior Earthdog (SE) must do a third part—to leave the den on command. The Master Earthdog (ME) is a bit more complicated.

SCHUTZHUND

The German word "Schutzhund" translated to English means "Protection Dog." It is a fast growing competitive sport in the United States and has been popular in England since the early 1900s. Schutzhund was originally a test to determine which German Shepherds were quality dogs for breeding in Germany. It gives us the ability to test our dogs for correct temperament and working ability. Like every other dog sport, it requires teamwork between the handler and the dog.

Schutzhund training and showing involves three phases: Tracking, Obedience, and Protection. There are three SchH levels: SchH I (novice), SchH II (intermediate), and SchH III (advanced). Each title becomes progressively more difficult. The handler and dog start out in each phase with 100 points. Points are deducted as errors are incurred. A total perfect score is 300, and for a dog and handler to earn a title he must earn at least 70 points in tracking and obedience and at least 80 points in protection. Today many different breeds participate successfully in Schutzhund.

GENERAL INFORMATION

Obedience, tracking, and agility allow the purebred dog with an Indefinite Listing Privilege (ILP) number or a limited registration to be exhibited and earn titles. Application must be made to the AKC for an ILP number.

The American Kennel Club publishes a monthly *Events* magazine that is part of the *Gazette*, their official journal for the sport of purebred dogs. The *Events* section lists upcoming shows and the secretary or superintendent for them. The majority of the conformation shows in the US are overseen by licensed superintendents. Generally the entry closing date is approximately two-and-a-half weeks before the actual show. Point shows are fairly expensive, while the match shows cost about one third of the point show entry fee. Match shows usually take entries the day of the show but some are pre-entry. The best way to find match show information is through your local kennel club. Upon asking, the AKC can provide you with a list of superintendents, and you can write and ask to be put on their mailing lists.

Obedience trial and tracking test information is available through the AKC. Frequently these events are not superintended, but put on by the host club. Therefore, you would make the entry with the event's secretary.

As you have read, there are numerous activities you can share with your dog. Regardless what you do, it does take teamwork. Your dog can only benefit from your attention and training. We hope this chapter has enlightened you and hope, if nothing else, you will attend a show here and there. Perhaps you will start with a puppy kindergarten class, and who knows where it may lead!

Ch. Classy Staffy Pardon Me Boys, OA, JWW, NAC, NAJ, NAG, FDCh., CGC, is an example of a well-rounded and versatile Staffordshire Bull Terrier.

HEALTH CARE

V eterinary medicine has become far more sophisticated than what was available to our ancestors. This can be attributed to the increase in household pets and consequently the demand for better care for them. Also human medicine has become far more complex. Today diagnostic testing in veterinary medicine parallels human diagnostics. Because of better technology we can expect our pets to live healthier lives, thereby, increasing their life spans.

THE FIRST CHECKUP

You will want to take your new puppy/dog in for his first checkup within 48 to 72 hours after acquiring it. Many breeders strongly recommend this checkup and so do the humane shelters. A puppy/dog can appear healthy but it may have a serious problem that is not apparent to the layman. Most pets have some type of a minor flaw

For the first few weeks of life, puppies receive immunization from nursing. Once weaned, they must receive vaccinations to protect them against diseases.

Dogs can pick up diseases from other dogs. Make sure your Staffordshire has all his vaccinations before taking him out to play with friends. that may never cause a real problem.

Unfortunately if he/she should have a serious problem, you will want to consider the consequences of keeping the pet and the attachments that will be formed, which may be broken prematurely. Keep in mind there are many healthy dogs looking for good homes.

This first checkup is a good time to establish yourself with the veterinarian and learn the office policy regarding their hours and how they handle emergencies. Usually the breeder or another conscientious pet owner is a good reference for locating a capable veterinarian. You should be aware that not all veterinarians give the same quality of service. Please do not make your selection on the least expensive clinic, as they may be shortchanging your pet. There is the possibility that eventually it will cost you more due to improper diagnosis, treatment, etc. If you are selecting a new veterinarian, feel free to ask for a tour of the clinic. You should inquire about making an appointment for a tour because all clinics are working clinics, and therefore may not be available all day for sightseers. You may worry less if you see where your pet will be spending the day if he ever needs to be hospitalized.

Regular health maintenance will ensure that your Staffordshire Bull Terrier leads a long and fruitful life.

THE PHYSICAL EXAM

Your veterinarian will check your pet's overall condition, which includes listening to the heart; checking the respiration; feeling the abdomen, muscles and joints; checking the mouth, which includes the gum color and signs of gum disease along with plaque buildup; checking the ears for signs of an infection or ear mites; examining the eyes; and, last but not least, checking the condition of the skin and coat.

He should ask you questions regarding your pet's eating and elimination habits and invite you to relay your questions. It is a good idea to prepare a list so as not to forget anything. He should discuss the proper diet and the quantity to be fed. If this should differ from your breeder's recommendation, then you should convey to him the breeder's choice and see if he approves. If he recommends changing the diet, then this should be done over a few days so as not to cause a gastrointestinal upset. It is customary to take in a fresh stool sample (just a small amount) for a test for intestinal parasites. It must be fresh, preferably within 12 hours, because the eggs hatch quickly and after hatching will not be observed under the microscope. If your pet isn't obliging then, usually the technician can take one in the clinic.

Although generally a hardy, healthy breed, there are certain diseases to which your Staffordshire can be vulnerable.

IMMUNIZATIONS

It is important that you take your puppy/dog's vaccination record with you on your first visit. In the case of a puppy, presumably the breeder has seen to the vaccinations up to the time you acquired custody. Veterinarians differ in their vaccination protocol. It is not unusual for your puppy to have received vaccinations for distemper, hepatitis, leptospirosis, parvovirus, and parainfluenza every two to three weeks from the age of five or six weeks. Usually this is a combined injection and is typically called the DHLPP. The DHLPP is given through at least 12 to 14 weeks of age, and it is customary to continue with another parvovirus vaccine at 16 to 18 weeks. You may wonder why so many immunizations are necessary. No one knows for sure when the puppy's maternal antibodies are gone, although it is customarily accepted that distemper antibodies are gone by 12 weeks. Usually parvovirus antibodies are gone by 16 to 18 weeks of age. However, it is possible for the maternal antibodies to be gone at a much earlier age or even a later age. Therefore, immunizations are started at an early age. The vaccine will not give immunity as long as there are maternal antibodies.

The rabies vaccination is given at three or six months of age depending on your local laws. A vaccine for bordetella (kennel cough) is advisable and can be given anytime from the age of five weeks. The coronavirus is not commonly given unless there is a problem locally. The Lyme vaccine is necessary in endemic areas. Lyme disease has been reported in 47 states.

Distemper

This is virtually an incurable disease. If the dog recovers, he is subject to severe nervous disorders. The virus attacks every tissue in the body and resembles a bad cold with a fever. It can cause a runny nose and eyes and cause gastrointestinal disorders, including a poor appetite, vomiting, and diarrhea. The virus is carried by raccoons, foxes, wolves, mink, and other dogs. Unvaccinated youngsters and senior citizens are very susceptible. This is still a common disease.

Hepatitis

This is a virus that is most serious in very young dogs. It is spread by contact with an infected animal or its stool or urine. The virus affects the liver and kidneys and is characterized by high fever, depression, and lack of appetite. Recovered animals may be afflicted with chronic illnesses.

Leptospirosis

This is a bacterial disease transmitted by contact with the urine of an infected dog, rat, or other wildlife. It produces severe symptoms of fever, depression, jaundice, and internal bleeding and was fatal before the vaccine was developed. Recovered dogs can be carriers, and the disease can be transmitted from dogs to humans.

Parvovirus

This was first noted in the late 1970s and is still a fatal disease. However, with proper vaccinations, early diagnosis and prompt treatment, it is a manageable disease. It attacks the bone marrow and intestinal tract. The symptoms include depression, loss of appetite, vomiting, diarrhea, and collapse. Immediate medical attention is of the essence.

Rabies

This is shed in the saliva and is carried by raccoons, skunks, foxes, other dogs, and cats. It attacks nerve tissue, resulting in paralysis and death. Rabies can be transmitted to people and is virtually always fatal. This disease is reappearing in the suburbs.

Bordetella (Kennel Cough)

The symptoms are coughing, sneezing, hacking, and retching accompanied by nasal discharge usually lasting from a few days to several weeks. There are several disease-producing organisms responsible for this disease. The present vaccines are helpful but do not protect for all the strains. It usually is not life threatening but in some instances it can progress to a serious bronchopneumonia. The disease is highly contagious. The vaccination should be given routinely for dogs that come in contact with other dogs, such as through boarding, training class, or visits to the groomer.

Bordetella attached to canine cilia. Otherwise known as kennel cough, this disease is highly contagious and should be vaccinated against routinely.

Coronavirus

This is usually self limiting and not life threatening. It was first noted in the late '70s about a year before parvovirus. The virus produces a yellow/brown stool and there may be depression, vomiting, and diarrhea.

Lyme Disease

This was first diagnosed in the United States in 1976 in Lyme, CT, in people who lived in close proximity to the deer tick. Symptoms may include acute lameness, fever, swelling of joints, and loss of appetite. Your veterinarian can advise you if you live in an endemic area.

After your puppy has completed his puppy vaccinations, you will continue to booster the DHLPP once a year. It is customary to booster the rabies one year after the first vaccine and then, depending on where you live, it should be boostered every year or every three years. This depends on your local laws. The Lyme and corona vaccines are boostered annually and it is recommended that the bordetella be boostered every six to eight months.

ANNUAL VISIT

I would like to impress the importance of the annual check-up, which would include the booster vaccinations, check for intestinal parasites, and test for heartworm. Today, in our very busy world it is rush, rush, and see "how much you can get for how little." Unbelievably, some non-veterinary businesses have entered into the vaccination business. More harm than good can come to your dog through improper vaccinations, possibly from inferior vaccines and/or the wrong schedule. More than likely you truly care about your companion dog and over the years you have devoted much time and expense to his well-being. Perhaps you are unaware that a vaccination is not just a vaccination. There is more involved. Please, please follow through with regular physical examinations. It is so important for your veterinarian to know your dog and this is especially true during middle age through the geriatric years. More than likely your older dog will require more than one physical a year. The annual physical is good preventive medicine. Through early diagnosis and subsequent treatment your dog can maintain a longer and better quality of life.

Whipworms are hard to find, and it is a job best left to a veterinarian.

INTESTINAL PARASITES

Hookworms

These are almost microscopic intestinal worms that can cause anemia and therefore, serious problems, including death, in young puppies. Hookworms can be transmitted to humans through penetration of the skin. Puppies may be born with them.

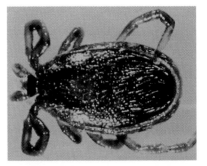

The deer tick is the most common carrier of Lyme disease. Photo courtesy of Virbac Laboratories, Inc., Fort Worth, Texas.

Roundworms

These are spaghetti-like worms that can cause a potbellied appearance and dull coat along with more severe symptoms, such as vomiting, diarrhea, and coughing. Puppies acquire these while in the mother's uterus and through lactation. Both hookworms and roundworms may be acquired through ingestion.

Whipworms

These have a three-month life cycle and are not acquired through the dam. They cause intermittent diarrhea usually with mucus. Whipworms are possibly the most difficult worm to eradicate. Their eggs are very resistant to most environmental factors and can last for years until the proper conditions enable them to mature. Whipworms are seldom seen in the stool.

Intestinal parasites are more prevalent in some areas than others. Climate, soil, and contamination are big factors contributing to the incidence of intestinal parasites. Eggs are passed in the stool, lay on the ground, and then become infective in a certain number of days. Each of the above worms has a different life cycle. Your best chance of becoming and remaining worm-free is to always pooper-scoop your yard. A fenced-in yard keeps stray dogs out, which is certainly helpful.

I would recommend having a fecal examination on your dog twice a year or more often if there is a problem. If your dog has a positive fecal sample, then he will be given the appropriate medication and you will be asked to bring back another stool sample in a certain period of time (depending on the type of worm) and then be rewormed. This process goes on until he has at least two negative samples. The different types of worms require different medications. You will be wasting your money and doing your dog an injustice by buying over-the-counter medication without first consulting your veterinarian.

OTHER INTERNAL PARASITES

Coccidiosis and Giardiasis

These protozoal infections usually affect puppies, especially in places where large numbers of puppies are brought together. Older dogs may harbor these infections but do not show signs unless they are stressed. Symptoms include diarrhea, weight loss, and lack of appetite. These infections are not always apparent in the fecal examination.

Tapeworms

Seldom apparent on fecal floatation, they are diagnosed frequently as rice-like segments around the dog's anus and the base of the tail. Tapeworms are long, flat and ribbon like, sometimes several feet in length, and made up of many segments about five-eighths of an inch long. The two most common types of tapeworms found in the dog are:

(1) First the larval form of the flea tapeworm parasite must mature in an intermediate host, the flea, before it can become infective. Your dog acquires this by ingesting the flea through licking and chewing.

(2) Rabbits, rodents, and certain large game animals serve as intermediate hosts for other species of tapeworms. If your dog should eat one of these infected hosts, then he can acquire tapeworms.

HEARTWORM DISEASE

This is a worm that resides in the heart and adjacent blood vessels of the lung that produces microfilaria, which circulate in the bloodstream. It is possible for a dog to be infected with any number of worms from one to a hundred that can be 6 to 14 inches long. It is a life-threatening disease, expensive to treat, and easily prevented. Depending on where you live, your veterinarian may recommend a preventive year-round and either an annual or semiannual blood test. The most common preventive is given once a month.

EXTERNAL PARASITES

Fleas

These pests are not only the dog's worst enemy but also enemy to the owner's pocketbook. Preventing is less expensive than treating, but regardless we'd prefer to spend our money elsewhere. Likely, the majority of our dogs are allergic to the bite of a flea, and in many cases it only takes one flea bite. The protein in the flea's saliva is the culprit. Allergic dogs have a reaction, which usually results in a "hot spot." More than likely such a reaction will involve a trip to the veterinarian for treatment. Yes, prevention is less expensive. Fortunately today there are several good products available.

If there is a flea infestation, no one product is going to correct the problem. Not only will the dog require treatment so will the environment. In general flea collars are not very effective although there is now available an "egg" collar that will kill the eggs on the dog. Dips are the most economical but they are messy. There are some effective shampoos and treatments available

Puppies need a lot of care, and your Staffordshire Bull Terrier will look to you, his owner, to take care of all his needs.

through pet shops and veterinarians. An oral tablet arrived on the American market in 1995 and was popular in Europe the previous year. It sterilizes the female flea but will not kill adult fleas. Therefore, the tablet, which is given monthly, will decrease the flea population but is not a "cure-all." Those dogs that suffer from flea-bite allergy will still be subjected to the bite of the flea. Another popular parasiticide is permethrin, which is applied to the back of the dog in one or two places depending on the dog's weight. This product works as a repellent causing the flea to get "hot feet" and jump off. Do not confuse this product with some of the organophosphates that are also applied to the dog's back.

Some products are not usable on young puppies. Treating fleas should be done under your veterinarian's guidance. Frequently it is necessary to combine products and the layman does not have the knowledge regarding possible toxicities. It is hard to believe but there are a few dogs that do have a natural resistance to fleas. Nevertheless it would be wise to treat all pets at the same time. Don't forget your cats. Cats just love to prowl the neighborhood and consequently return with unwanted guests.

If your puppy experiences a change in personality or seems listless, take him to the veterinarian immediately.

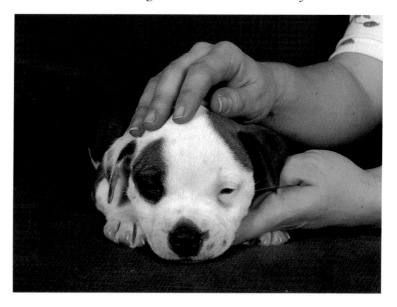

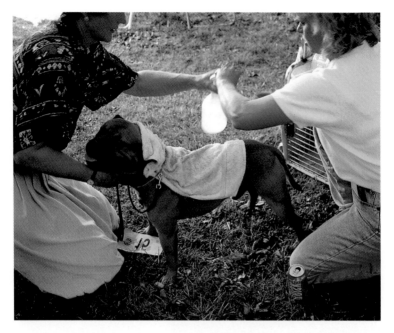

Staffordshire Bull Terriers can have an adverse reaction to the heat, so be sure to keep your dog cool and comfortable at all times.

Adult fleas live on the dog but their eggs drop off the dog into the environment. There they go through four larval stages before reaching adulthood, and thereby are able to jump back on the poor unsuspecting dog. The cycle resumes and takes between 21 to 28 days under ideal conditions. There are environmental products available that will kill both the adult fleas and the larvae.

Ticks

Ticks carry Rocky Mountain Spotted Fever, Lyme disease, and can cause tick paralysis. They should be removed with tweezers, trying to pull out the head. The jaws carry disease. There is a tick preventive collar that does an excellent job. The ticks automatically back out on those dogs wearing collars.

Sarcoptic Mange

This is a mite that is difficult to find on skin scrapings. The pinnal reflex is a good indicator of this disease. Rub the ends of the pinna (ear) together and the dog will start scratching with his foot. Sarcoptes are highly contagious to other dogs and to humans although they do not live long on humans. They cause intense itching.

Demodectic Mange
This is a mite that is passed from the dam to her puppies. It affects youngsters age three to ten months. Diagnosis is confirmed by skin scraping. Small areas of alopecia around the eyes, lips, and/or forelegs become visible. There is little itching unless there is a secondary bacterial infection. Some breeds are afflicted more than others.

Your Staffordshire can pick up parasites like fleas and ticks when outdoors. Make sure to check his coat thoroughly after playing outside.

Cheyletiella
This causes intense itching and is diagnosed by skin scraping. It lives in the outer layers of the skin of dogs, cats, rabbits, and humans. Yellow-gray scales may be found on the back and the rump, top of the head, and the nose.

To Breed or Not To Breed
More than likely your breeder has requested that you have your puppy neutered or spayed. Your breeder's request is based on what is healthiest for your dog and what is most beneficial for your breed. Experienced and conscientious breeders devote many years into developing a bloodline. In order to do this, he makes every effort to plan each breeding in regard to conformation, temperament, and health. This type of breeder does his best to perform the necessary testing (i.e., OFA, CERF, testing for inherited blood disorders, thyroid, etc.). Testing is expensive and sometimes very disheartening when a favorite dog doesn't pass his health tests. The health history

pertains not only to the breeding stock but to the immediate ancestors. Reputable breeders do not want their offspring to be bred indiscriminately. Therefore, you may be asked to neuter or spay your puppy. Of course there is always the exception, and your breeder may agree to let you breed your dog under his direct supervision. This is an important concept. More and more effort is being made to breed healthier dogs.

Spay/Neuter

There are numerous benefits of performing this surgery at six months of age. Unspayed females are subject to mammary and ovarian cancer. In order to prevent mammary cancer she must be spayed prior to her first heat cycle. Later in life, an unspayed female may develop a pyometra (an infected uterus), which is definitely life threatening.

Spaying is performed under a general anesthetic and is easy on the young dog. As you might expect it is a little harder on the older dog, but that is no reason to deny her the surgery. The surgery removes the ovaries and uterus. It is important to remove all the ovarian tissue. If some is left behind, she could remain attractive to males. In order to view the ovaries, a reasonably long incision is necessary. An ovariohysterectomy is considered major surgery.

Neutering the male at a young age will inhibit some characteristic male behavior that owners frown upon. Some boys will not hike their legs and mark territory if they are neutered at six months of age. Also neutering at a young age has hormonal benefits, lessening the chance of hormonal aggressiveness.

Spaying or neutering your dog will not only prevent certain diseases, but will help control the pet population.

Surgery involves removing the testicles but leaving the scrotum. If there should be a retained testicle, then he definitely needs to be neutered before the age of two or three years. Retained testicles can develop into cancer. Unneutered males are at risk for testicular cancer, perineal fistulas, perianal tumors and fistulas, and prostatic disease. Intact males and females are prone to housebreaking accidents. Females urinate frequently before, during, and after heat cycles, and males tend to mark territory if there is a female in heat. Males may show the same behavior if there is a visiting dog or guests.

Surgery involves a sterile operating procedure equivalent to human surgery. The incision site is shaved, surgically scrubbed and draped. The veterinarian wears a sterile surgical gown, cap, mask, and gloves. Anesthesia should be monitored by a registered technician. It is customary for the veterinarian to recommend a pre-anesthetic blood screening, looking for metabolic problems and a ECG rhythm strip to check for normal heart function. Today anesthetics are equal to human anesthetics, which enables your dog to walk out of the clinic the same day as surgery.

Some folks worry about their dog gaining weight after being neutered or spayed. This is usually not the case. It is true that some dogs may be less active so they could develop a problem, but most dogs are just as active as they were before surgery. However, if your dog should begin to gain, then you need to decrease his food and see to it that he gets a little more exercise.

MEDICAL PROBLEMS

Anal Sacs

These are small sacs on either side of the rectum that can cause the dog discomfort when they are full. They should empty when the dog has a bowel movement. Symptoms of inflammation or impaction are excessive licking under the tail and/or a bloody or sticky discharge from the anal area. Breeders like myself recommend emptying the sacs on a regular schedule when bathing the dog. Many veterinarians prefer this isn't done unless there are symptoms. You can express the sacs by squeezing the two sacs (at the five and seven o'clock positions) in and up toward the anus. Take precautions not to get in the way of the foul-smelling fluid that is expressed. Some dogs object to this procedure so it would be wise to have someone hold the head. Scooting is caused by anal-sac irritation and not worms.

Colitis

The stool may be frank blood or blood tinged and is the result of inflammation of the colon. Colitis, sometimes intermittent, can be the result of stress, undiagnosed whipworms, or perhaps idiopathic (no explainable reason). If intermittent bloody stools are an ongoing problem, you should probably feed a diet higher in fiber. Seek professional help if your dog feels poorly and/or the condition persists.

Conjunctivitis

Many breeds are prone to this problem. The conjunctiva is the pink tissue that lines the inner surface of the eyeball except the clear, transparent cornea. Irritating substances such as bacteria, foreign matter, or chemicals can cause it to become reddened and swollen. It is important to keep any hair trimmed from around the eyes. Long hair stays damp and aggravates the problem. Keep the eyes cleaned with warm water and wipe away any matter that has accumulated in the corner of the eyes. If the condition persists, you should see your veterinarian. This problem goes hand in hand with keratoconjunctivitis sicca.

Some breeders will sell pet-quality Staffordshire Bull Terrier pups on the condition that they are spayed or neutered.

DENTAL CARE for Your Dog's Life

So you've got a new puppy! You also have a new set of puppy teeth in your household. Anyone who has ever raised a puppy is abundantly aware of these new teeth. Your puppy will chew anything he can reach, chase your shoelaces, and play "tear the rag" with any piece of clothing he can find. When puppies are newly born, they have no teeth. At about four weeks of age, puppies of most breeds begin to develop their deciduous or baby teeth. They begin eating semi-solid food, fighting and biting with their litter mates, and learning discipline from their mother. As their new teeth come in, they inflict more pain on their mother's breasts, so her feeding sessions become less frequent and shorter. By six or eight weeks, the mother will start growling to warn her pups when they are fighting too roughly or hurting her as they nurse too much with their new teeth.

Chew toys, like Nylabones®, can help your Staffordshire exercise his teeth and gums, as well as help keep your belongings safe.

Puppies need to chew. It is a necessary part of their physical and mental development. They develop muscles and necessary life skills as they drag objects around, fight over possession, and vocalize alerts and warnings. Puppies chew on things to explore their world. They are using their sense of taste to determine what is food and what is not. How else can they tell an electrical cord from a lizard? At about four months of age, most puppies begin shedding their baby teeth. Often these teeth need some help to come out and make way for the permanent teeth. The incisors (front teeth) will be replaced first. Then, the adult canine or fang teeth erupt. When the baby tooth is not shed before the permanent tooth comes in, veterinarians call it a retained deciduous tooth. This condition will often cause gum infections by trapping hair and debris between the permanent tooth and the retained baby tooth. Nylafloss® is an excellent device for puppies to use. They can toss it, drag it, and chew on the many surfaces it presents. The

baby teeth can catch in the nylon material, aiding in their removal. Puppies that have adequate chew toys will have less destructive behavior, develop more physically, and have less chance of retained deciduous teeth.

During the first year, your dog should be seen by your veterinarian at regular intervals. Your veterinarian will let you know when to bring in your puppy for vaccinations and parasite examinations. At each visit, your veterinarian should inspect the lips, teeth, and mouth as part of a complete physical examination. You should take some part in the maintenance of your dog's oral health. You should examine your dog's mouth weekly throughout his first year to make sure there are no sores, foreign objects, tooth problems, etc. If your dog drools excessively, shakes his head, or has bad breath, consult your veterinarian. By the time your dog is six months old, the permanent teeth are all in and plaque can start to accumulate on the tooth surfaces. This is when your dog needs to develop good dental-care habits to prevent calculus build-up on his teeth. Brushing is best. That is a fact

A thorough oral inspection and teeth cleaning should be a part of your Staffordshire's regular grooming routine.

128

Providing your Staffordshire pup with plenty of safe toys to chew on will help him keep his teeth healthy.

that cannot be denied. However, some dogs do not like their teeth brushed regularly, or you may not be able to accomplish the task. In that case, you should consider a product that will help prevent plaque and calculus build-up.

The Plaque Attackers® and Galileo Bone® are other excellent choices for the first three years of a dog's life. Their shapes make them interesting for the dog. As the dog chews on them, the solid polyurethane massages the gums, which improves the blood circulation to the periodontal tissues. Projections on the chew devices increase the surface and are in contact with the tooth for more efficient cleaning. The unique shape and consistency prevent your dog from exerting excessive force on his own teeth or from breaking off pieces of the bone. If your dog is an aggressive chewer or weighs more than 55 pounds (25 kg), you should consider giving him a Nylabone®, the most durable chew product on the market.

The Gumabones ®, made by the Nylabone Company, is constructed of strong polyurethane, which is softer than nylon. Less powerful chewers prefer the Gumabones® to the

Nylabones®. A super option for your dog is the Hercules Bone®, a uniquely shaped bone named after the great Olympian for its exceptional strength. Like all Nylabone products, they are specially scented to make them attractive to your dog. Ask your veterinarian about these bones and he will validate the good doctor's prescription: Nylabones® not only give your dog a good chewing workout but also help to save your dog's teeth (and even his life, as it protects him from possible fatal periodontal diseases).

By the time dogs are four years old, 75 percent of them have periodontal disease. It is the most common infection in dogs. Yearly examinations by your veterinarian are essential to maintaining your dog's good health. If your veterinarian detects periodontal disease, he or she may recommend a prophylactic cleaning. To do a thorough cleaning, it will be necessary to put your dog under anesthesia. With modern gas anesthetics and monitoring equipment, the procedure is pretty safe. Your veterinarian will scale the teeth with an ultrasound scaler or hand instrument. This removes the calculus from the teeth. If there are calculus deposits below the gum line, the veterinarian will plane the roots to make them smooth. After all of the calculus has been removed, the teeth are polished with pumice in a polishing cup. If any medical or surgical treatment is needed, it is done at this time. The final step would be fluoride treatment and your follow-up treatment at home. If the periodontal disease is advanced, the veterinarian may prescribe a medicated mouth rinse or antibiotics for use at home. Make sure your dog has safe, clean and attractive chew toys and treats. Chooz® treats are another way of using a consumable treat to help keep your dog's teeth clean.

Rawhide is the most popular of all materials for a dog to chew. This has never been good news to dog owners, because rawhide is inherently very dangerous for dogs. Thousands of dogs have died from rawhide, having swallowed the hide after it has become soft and mushy, only to cause stomach and intestinal blockage. A new rawhide product on the market has finally solved the problem of rawhide: molded Roar-Hide® from Nylabone. These

Staffordshire Bull Terriers have strong jaws and chewing power, so get them toys that are tough and that will not break into small pieces.

are composed of processed, cut up, and melted American rawhide injected into your dog's favorite shape: a dog bone. These dog-safe devices smell and taste like rawhide but don't break up. The ridges on the bones help to fight tartar build-up on the teeth and they last ten times longer than the usual rawhide chews.

As your dog ages, professional examination and cleaning should become more frequent. The mouth should be inspected at least once a year. Your veterinarian may recommend visits every six months. In the geriatric patient, organs such as the heart, liver, and kidneys do not function as well as when they were young. Your veterinarian will probably want to test these organs' functions prior to using general anesthesia for dental cleaning. If your dog is a good chewer and you work closely with your veterinarian, your dog can keep all of his teeth all of his life.

If you give your dog good dental care during his lifetime, he will always be able to flash a healthy smile.

Chew toys can also be used as rewards in training sessions. This Staffordshire will do anything to get his Nylabone®.

However, as your dog ages, his sense of smell, sight, and taste will diminish. He may not have the desire to chase, trap or chew his toys. He will also not have the energy to chew for long periods, as arthritis and periodontal disease make chewing painful. This will leave you with more responsibility for keeping his teeth clean and healthy. The dog that would not let you brush his teeth at one year of age may let you brush his teeth now that he is ten years old.

If you train your dog with good chewing habits as a puppy, he will have healthier teeth throughout his life.

TRAVELING with Your Dog

The earlier you start traveling with your new puppy or dog, the better. He needs to become accustomed to traveling. However, some dogs are nervous riders and become carsick easily. It is helpful if he starts with an empty stomach. Do not despair, as it will go better if you continue taking him with you on short fun rides. How would you feel if every time you rode in the car you stopped at the doctor's for an injection? You would soon dread that nasty car. Older dogs that tend to get carsick may have more of a problem adjusting to traveling. Those dogs that are having a serious problem may benefit from some medication prescribed by the veterinarian.

Day Dream Dancing Barefoot, at nine weeks of age, looks ready to go.

Do give your dog a chance to relieve himself before getting into the car. It is a good idea to be prepared for a clean up with a leash, paper towels, bag, and terry cloth towel.

The safest place for your dog is in a fiberglass crate, although close confinement can promote carsickness in some dogs. If your dog is nervous you can try letting him ride on the seat next to you or in someone's lap.

An alternative to the crate would be to use a car harness made for dogs and/or a safety strap attached to the harness or collar. Whatever you do, do not let your dog ride in the back of a pickup truck unless he is securely tied on a very short lead. I've seen trucks stop quickly and, even though the dog was tied, he fell out and was dragged.

Another advantage of the crate is that it is a safe place to leave him if you need to run into the store. Otherwise you

Crates are the safest way for your Staffordshire Bull Terrier to travel in the car.

wouldn't be able to leave the windows down. Keep in mind that while many dogs are overly protective in their crates, this may not be enough to deter dognappers. In some states it is against the law to leave a dog in the car unattended.

Never leave a dog loose in the car wearing a collar and leash. More than one dog has killed himself by hanging. Do not let him put his head out an open window. Foreign debris can be blown into his eyes. When leaving your dog unattended in a car, consider the temperature. It can take less than five minutes to reach temperatures over 100 degrees Fahrenheit.

A boarding kennel is an option for your Staffordshire if he cannot accompany you on trips.

TRIPS

Perhaps you are taking a trip. Give consideration to what is best for your dog–traveling with you or boarding. When traveling by car, van, or motor home, you need to think ahead about locking your vehicle. In all probability you have many valuables in the car and do not wish to leave it unlocked. Perhaps most valuable and not replaceable is your dog. Give thought to securing your vehicle and providing adequate ventilation for him. Another consideration for you when traveling with your dog is medical problems that may arise and little inconveniences, such as exposure to external parasites. Some areas of the country are quite flea infested. You may want to carry flea spray with you. This is even a good idea when staying in motels. Quite possibly you are not the only occupant of the room.

Unbelievably many motels and even hotels do allow canine guests, even some very first-class ones. Gaines Pet Foods Corporation publishes *Touring With Towser*, a directory of domestic hotels and motels that accommodate guests with dogs. Their address is Gaines TWT, PO Box 5700, Kankakee, IL, 60902. Call ahead to any motel that you may be considering and see if they accept pets. Sometimes it is necessary to pay a deposit against room damage. The management may feel reassured if you mention that your dog will be crated. If you do travel with your dog, take along plenty of baggies so that you can clean up after him. When we all do our share in cleaning up, we make it possible for motels to continue accepting our pets. As a matter of fact, you should practice cleaning up everywhere you take your dog.

Staffordshires that compete in dog shows must become accustomed to extensive traveling.

Depending on where your are traveling, you may need an up-to-date health certificate issued by your veterinarian. It is good policy to take along your dog's medical information, which would include the name, address and phone number of your veterinarian, vaccination record, rabies certificate, and any medication he is taking.

AIR TRAVEL

When traveling by air, you need to contact the airlines to check their policy. Usually you have to make arrangements up to a couple of weeks in advance for traveling with your dog. The airlines require your dog to travel in an airline approved fiberglass crate. Usually these can be purchased through the airlines but they are also readily available in most pet-supply stores. If your dog is not accustomed to a crate, then it is a good idea to get him acclimated to it before your trip. The day of the actual trip you should withhold water about one hour ahead of departure and no food for about 12 hours. The airlines generally have temperature restrictions, which do not allow pets to travel if it is either too cold or too hot. Frequently these restrictions are based on the temperatures at the departure and arrival airports. It's best to inquire about a health certificate. These usually need to be issued within ten days of departure. You should arrange for non-stop, direct flights and if a commuter plane should be involved, check to see if it will carry dogs. Some don't. The Humane Society of the United States has put together a tip sheet for airline traveling. You can receive a copy by sending a self-addressed stamped envelope to:

The Humane Society of the United States
Tip Sheet
2100 L Street NW
Washington, DC 20037.

Regulations differ for traveling outside of the country and are sometimes changed without notice. Well in advance you need to write or call the appropriate consulate or agricultural department for instructions. Some countries have lengthy quarantines (six months), and countries differ in their rabies vaccination requirements. For instance, it may have to be given at least 30 days ahead of your departure.

Do make sure your dog is wearing proper identification including your name, phone number, and city. You never know when you might be in an accident and separated from your dog. Or your dog could be frightened and somehow manage to escape and run away.

Another suggestion would be to carry in-case-of-emergency instructions. These would include the address and phone number of a relative or friend, your veterinarian's name, address and phone number, and your dog's medical information.

BOARDING KENNELS

Perhaps you have decided that you need to board your dog. Your veterinarian can recommend a good boarding facility or possibly a pet sitter that will come to your house. It is customary for the boarding kennel to ask for proof of vaccination for the DHLPP, rabies, and bordetella vaccine. The bordetella should have been given within six months of boarding. This is for your protection. If they do not ask for this proof I would not board at their kennel. Ask about flea control. Those dogs that suffer flea-bite allergy can get in trouble at a boarding kennel. Unfortunately boarding kennels are limited on how much they are able to do.

For more information on pet sitting, contact NAPPS:
National Association of Professional Pet Sitters
1200 G Street, NW
Suite 760
Washington, DC 20005.

Some pet clinics have technicians that pet sit and technicians that board clinic patients in their homes. This may be an alternative for you. Ask your veterinarian if they have an employee that can help you. There is a definite advantage of having a technician care for your dog, especially if your dog is on medication or is a senior citizen.

Staffordshire Bull Terriers are happiest when allowed to participate in family activities, including traveling. These two Stafs don't want to be left out of anything.

You can write for a copy of *Traveling With Your Pet* from ASPCA, Education Department, 441 E. 92nd Street, New York, NY 10128.

IDENTIFICATION and Finding the Lost Dog

There are several ways of identifying your dog. The old standby is a collar with dog license, rabies, and ID tags. Unfortunately collars have a way of being separated from the dog and tags fall off. We're not suggesting you shouldn't use a collar and tags. If they stay intact and on the dog, they are the quickest way of identification.

For several years owners have been tattooing their dogs. Some tattoos use a number with a registry. Here lies the problem because there are several registries to check. If you wish to tattoo, use your social security number. The humane shelters have the means to trace it. It is usually done on the inside of the rear thigh. The area is first shaved and numbed. There is no pain, although a few dogs do not like the buzzing

Your Staffordshire should wear his collar and identification tags at all times in case he should become separated from you.

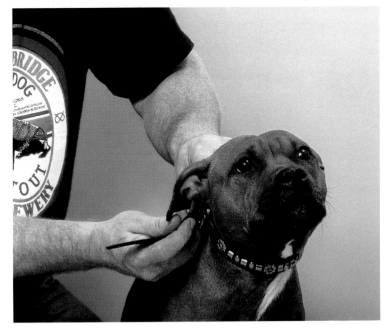

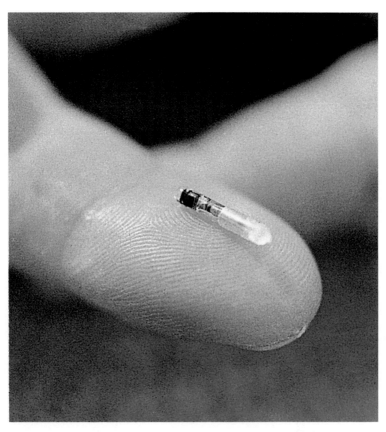

The newest method of identification is the microchip, a computer chip no bigger than a grain of rice that is injected into a dog's skin.

sound. Occasionally tattooing is not legible and needs to be redone.

The newest method of identification is microchipping. The microchip is a computer chip that is no larger than a grain of rice. The veterinarian implants it by injection between the shoulder blades. The dog feels no discomfort. If your dog is lost and picked up by the humane society, they can trace you by scanning the microchip, which has its own code. Microchip scanners are friendly to other brands of microchips and their registries. The microchip comes with a dog tag saying the dog is microchipped. It is the safest way of identifying your dog.

FINDING THE LOST DOG

I am sure you will agree that there would be little worse than losing your dog. Responsible pet owners rarely lose their dogs. They do not let their dogs run free because they don't want harm to come to them. Not only that but in most, if not all, states there is a leash law.

Beware of fenced-in yards. They can be a hazard. Dogs find ways to escape either over or under the fence. Another fast exit is through the gate that perhaps the neighbor's child left unlocked.

Below is a list that hopefully will be of help to you if you need it. Remember don't give up, keep looking. Your dog is worth your efforts.

Your Staffordshire Bull Terrier should be in a safe, fenced-in enclosure if left outside unsupervised.

1. Contact your neighbors and put flyers with a photo on it in their mailboxes. Information you should include would be the dog's name, breed, sex, color, age, source of identification, when your dog was last seen and where, and your name and phone numbers. It may be helpful to say the dog needs medical care. Offer a *reward*.
2. Check all local shelters daily. It is also possible for your dog to be picked up away from home and end up in an out-of-the-way shelter. Check these, too. Go in person. It is not good enough to call. Most shelters are limited on the time they can hold dogs then they are put up for adoption or euthanized. There is the possibility that your dog will not make it to the shelter for several days. Your dog could have been wandering or someone may have tried to keep him.
3. Notify all local veterinarians. Call and send flyers.
4. Call your breeder. Frequently breeders are contacted when one of their breed is found.
5. Contact the rescue group for your breed.
6. Contact local schools—children may have seen your dog.
7. Post flyers at the schools, groceries, gas stations, convenience stores, veterinary clinics, groomers and any other place that will allow them.
8. Advertise in the newspaper.
9. Advertise on the radio.

BEHAVIOR and Canine Communication

Studies of the human/animal bond point out the importance of the unique relationships that exist between people and their pets. Those of us who share our lives with pets understand the special part they play through companionship, service, and protection. For many, the pet/owner bond goes beyond simple companionship; pets are often considered members of the family. A leading pet food manufacturer recently conducted a nationwide survey of pet owners to gauge just how important pets were in their lives. Here's what they found:

Many people thrive on the companionship that a Staffordshire Bull Terrier can provide.

- 76 percent allow their pets to sleep on their beds
- 78 percent think of their pets as their children
- 84 percent display photos of their pets, mostly in their homes
- 84 percent think that their pets react to their own emotions
- 100 percent talk to their pets
- 97 percent think that their pets understand what they're saying

Are you surprised?

Senior citizens show more concern for their own eating habits when they have the responsibility of feeding a dog. Seeing that the dog is routinely exercised encourages the owner to think of schedules that otherwise may seem unimportant to the senior citizen. The older owner may be arthritic and feeling poorly but with responsibility for his dog he has a reason to get up and get moving. It is a big plus if his dog is an attention seeker who will demand such from his owner.

Over the last couple of decades, it has been shown that pets relieve the stress of those who lead busy lives. Owning a pet has been known to lessen the occurrence of heart attack and stroke.

Many single folks thrive on the companionship of a dog. Lifestyles are very different from a long time ago, and today

more individuals seek the single life. However, they receive fulfillment from owning a dog.

Most likely the majority of our dogs live in family environments. The companionship they provide is well worth the effort involved. In my opinion, every child should have the opportunity to have a family dog. Dogs teach responsibility through understanding their care, feelings, and even respecting their life cycles. Frequently those children who have not been exposed to dogs grow up afraid of dogs, which isn't good. Dogs sense timidity and some will take advantage of the situation.

Dog ownership can help teach a child responsibility, love, and respect for animals. Int./Am. Ch. Slam Dance, CGC, with his friend Gaby.

Today more dogs are serving as service dogs. Since the origination of the Seeing Eye dogs years ago, we now have trained hearing dogs. Also dogs are trained to provide service for the handicapped and are able to perform many different tasks for their owners. Search and Rescue dogs, with their handlers, are sent throughout the world to assist in recovery of disaster victims. They are life savers.

Therapy dogs are very popular with nursing homes, and some hospitals even allow them to visit. The inhabitants truly look forward to their visits. They wanted and were allowed to have visiting dogs in their beds to hold and love.

Nationally there is a Pet Awareness Week to educate students and others about the value and basic care of our pets. Many countries take an even greater interest in their pets than Americans do. In those countries the pets are allowed to accompany their owners into restaurants and shops, etc. In the US this freedom is only available to our service dogs. Even so we think very highly of the human/animal bond.

Many people consider their Staffordshire to be a valued member of the family. Kersten Buschmann and her canine friends Dolly and Prime visit Santa.

CANINE BEHAVIOR

Canine behavior problems are the number-one reason for pet owners to dispose of their dogs, either through new homes, humane shelters, or euthanasia. Unfortunately there are too many owners who are unwilling to devote the necessary time to properly train their dogs. On the other hand, there are those who not only are concerned about inherited health problems but are also aware of the dog's mental stability.

You may realize that a breed and his group relatives (i.e., sporting, hounds, etc.) show tendencies to behavioral characteristics. An experienced breeder can acquaint you with his breed's personality. Unfortunately many breeds are labeled with poor temperaments when actually the breed as a whole is not affected but only a small percentage of individuals within the breed.

Inheritance and environment contribute to the dog's behavior. Some naïve people suggest inbreeding as the cause of bad temperaments. Inbreeding only results in poor behavior if the ancestors carry the trait. If there are excellent temperaments behind the dogs, then inbreeding will promote good temperaments in the offspring. Did you ever consider that inbreeding is what sets the characteristics of a breed? A purebred dog is the end result of inbreeding. This does not spare the mixed-breed dog from the same problems. Mixed-breed dogs frequently are the offspring of purebred dogs.

Not too many decades ago most of our dogs led a different lifestyle than what is prevalent today. Usually mom stayed home so the dog had human companionship and someone to discipline him if needed. Not much was expected from the dog. Today's mom works and everyone's life is at a much faster pace.

Early socialization with littermates will teach your Staffordshire that he has boundaries and limits to his behavior.

Socialization is very important for a well-adjusted Staffordshire. The dog may have to adjust to being a "weekend" dog. The family is gone all day during the week, and the dog is left to his own devices for entertainment. Some dogs sleep all day waiting for their family to come home and others become wigwam wreckers if given the opportunity. Crates do ensure the safety of the dog and the house. However, he could become a physically and emotionally cripple if he doesn't get enough exercise and attention. We still appreciate and want the companionship of our dogs although we expect more from them. In many cases we tend to forget dogs are just that—*dogs* not human beings.

SOCIALIZING AND TRAINING

Many prospective puppy buyers lack experience regarding the proper socialization and training needed to develop the type of pet we all desire. In the first 18 months, training does take some work. It is easier to start proper training before there is a problem that needs to be corrected.

The initial work begins with the breeder. The breeder should start socializing the puppy at five to six weeks of age and cannot let up. Human socializing is critical up through 12

At times your Staffordshire may question your authority, but he must always know that you are in charge in the relationship.

weeks of age and likewise important during the following months. The litter should be left together during the first few weeks but it is necessary to separate them by ten weeks of age. Leaving them together after that time will increase competition for litter dominance. If puppies are not socialized with people by 12 weeks of age, they will be timid in later life.

The eight- to ten-week age period is a fearful time for puppies. They need to be handled very gently around children and adults. There should be no harsh discipline during this time. Starting at 14 weeks of age, the puppy begins the juvenile period, which ends when he reaches sexual maturity around 6 to 14 months of age. During the juvenile period he needs to be introduced to strangers (adults, children and other dogs) on the home property. At sexual maturity he will begin to bark at strangers and become more protective. Males start to lift their legs to urinate but if you desire you can inhibit this behavior by walking your boy on leash away from trees, shrubs, fences, etc.

You can often tell what your Staffordshire is thinking or feeling by watching his body language.

Perhaps you are thinking about an older puppy. You need to inquire about the puppy's social experience. If he has lived in a kennel, he may have a hard time adjusting to people and environmental stimuli. Assuming he has had a good social upbringing, there are advantages to an older puppy.

Training includes puppy kindergarten and a minimum of one to two basic training classes. During these classes you will learn how to dominate your youngster. This is especially important if you own a large breed of dog. It is somewhat harder, if not nearly impossible, for some owners to be the Alpha figure when their dog towers over them. You will be taught how to restrain your dog properly. This concept is important. Again it puts you in the Alpha position. All dogs need to be restrained many times during their lives. Believe it or not, some of our worst offenders are the eight-week-old puppies that are brought to our clinic. They need to be gently restrained for a nail trim but the way they carry on you would think we were killing them. In comparison, their vaccination is a "piece of cake." When we ask dogs to do something that is not agreeable to them, then their worst comes out. Life will be easier for your dog if you expose him at a young age to the necessities of life—proper behavior and restraint.

UNDERSTANDING THE DOG'S LANGUAGE

Most authorities agree that the dog is a descendent of the wolf. The dog and wolf have similar traits. For instance both are pack oriented and prefer not to be isolated for long periods of time. Another characteristic is that the dog, like the wolf, looks to the leader—Alpha—for direction. Both the wolf and the dog communicate through body language, not only within their pack but with outsiders.

Every pack has an Alpha figure. The dog looks to you, or should look to you, to be that leader. If your dog doesn't receive the proper training and guidance, he very well may replace you as Alpha. This would be a serious problem and is certainly a disservice to your dog.

Eye contact is one way the Alpha wolf keeps order within his pack. You are Alpha so you must establish eye contact with your puppy. Obviously your puppy will have to look at you. Practice eye contact even if you need to hold his head for five to ten seconds at a time. You can give him a treat as a reward. Make sure your eye contact is gentle and not threatening. Later, if he has been naughty, it is permissible to give him a long, penetrating look. There are some older dogs that never learned eye contact as puppies and cannot accept eye contact. You should avoid eye contact with these dogs since they feel threatened and will retaliate as such.

BODY LANGUAGE

The play bow, when the forequarters are down and the hindquarters are elevated, is an invitation to play. Puppies play fight, which helps them learn the acceptable limits of biting. This is necessary for later in their lives. Nevertheless, an owner may be falsely reassured by the playful nature of his dog's aggression. Playful aggression toward another dog or human may be an indication of serious aggression in the future. Owners should never play fight or play tug-of-war with any dog that is inclined to be dominant.

Signs of submission are:

1. Avoids eye contact.
2. Active submission—the dog crouches down, ears back, and the tail is lowered.
3. Passive submission—the dog rolls on his side with his hindlegs in the air and frequently urinates.

Signs of dominance are:

1. Makes eye contact.
2. Stands with ears up, tail up, and the hair raised on his neck.
3. Shows dominance over another dog by standing at right angles over him.

Dominant dogs tend to behave in characteristic ways such as:

1. The dog may be unwilling to move from his place (i.e., reluctant to give up the sofa if the owner wants to sit there).

2. He may not part with toys or objects in his mouth and may

Even the sweetest-looking puppies can develop behavior problems. That is why it is important to be a firm and fair owner.

show possessiveness with his food bowl.

3. He may not respond quickly to commands.

4. He may be disagreeable for grooming and dislikes to be petted.

Dogs are popular because of their sociable nature. Those that have contact with humans during the first 12 weeks of life regard them as a member of their own species—their pack. All dogs have the potential for both dominant and submissive behavior. Only through experience and training do they learn to whom it is appropriate to show which behavior. Not all dogs are concerned with dominance but owners need to be aware of that potential. It is wise for the owner to establish his dominance early on.

A human can express dominance or submission toward a dog in the following ways:

1. Meeting the dog's gaze signals dominance. Averting the gaze signals submission. If the dog growls or threatens, averting the gaze is the first avoiding action to take—it may prevent attack. It is important to establish eye contact in the puppy. The older dog that has not been exposed to eye contact may see it as a threat and will not be willing to submit.

2. Being taller than the dog signals dominance; being lower signals submission. This is why, when attempting to make friends with a strange dog or catch the runaway, one should kneel down to his level. Some owners see their dogs become dominant when allowed on the furniture or on the bed. Then he is at the owner's level.

3. An owner can gain dominance by ignoring all the dog's social initiatives. The owner pays attention to the dog only when he obeys a command.

No dog should be allowed to achieve dominant status over any adult or child. Ways of preventing are as follows:

1. Handle the puppy gently, especially during the three- to four-month period.

Some dogs may jump up as a sign of affection, but your Staffordshire should learn to sit for petting and attention.

2. Let the children and adults handfeed him and teach him to take food without lunging or grabbing.

3. Do not allow him to chase children or joggers.

4. Do not allow him to jump on

people or mount their legs. Even females may be inclined to mount. It is not only a male habit.

5. Do not allow him to growl for any reason.

6. Don't participate in wrestling or tug-of-war games.

7. Don't physically punish puppies for aggressive behavior. Restrain him from repeating the infraction and teach an alternative behavior. Dogs should earn everything they receive from their owners. This would include sitting to receive petting or treats, sitting before going out the door, and sitting to receive the collar and leash. These types of exercises reinforce the owner's dominance.

Young children should never be left alone with a dog. It is important that children learn some basic obedience commands so they have some control over the dog. They will gain the respect of their dog.

Mischievous dogs can get into a lot of trouble if left unsupervised. This Staffordshire has gotten himself up and needs a little help getting down.

FEAR

One of the most common problems dogs experience is being fearful. Some dogs are more afraid than others. On the lesser side, which is sometimes humorous to watch, dogs can be afraid of a strange object. They act silly when something is out of place in the house. We call his problem perceptive intelligence. He realizes the abnormal within his known environment. He does not react the same way in strange environments because he does not know what is normal.

On the more serious side is a fear of people. This can result in backing off, seeking his own space, and saying "leave me alone" or it can result in an aggressive behavior that may lead to challenging the person. Respect that the dog wants to be left alone and give him time to come forward. If you approach the cornered dog, he may resort to snapping. If you leave him alone, he may decide to come forward, which should be rewarded with a treat.

Some dogs may initially be too fearful to take treats. In these cases it is helpful to make sure the dog hasn't eaten for about 24 hours. Being a little hungry encourages him to accept the treats, especially if they are of the "gourmet" variety.

Trouble is always lurking when there is a puppy in the house. Make sure your puppy is well supervised or confine him when you can't be with him.

Dogs can be afraid of numerous things, including loud noises and thunderstorms. Invariably the owner rewards (by comforting) the dog when he shows signs of fearfulness. When your dog is frightened, direct his attention to something else and act happy. Don't dwell on his fright.

AGGRESSION

Some different types of aggression are: predatory, defensive, dominance, possessive, protective, fear induced, noise provoked, "rage" syndrome (unprovoked aggression), maternal, and aggression directed toward other dogs. Aggression is the most common behavioral problem encountered. Protective breeds like the Stafford are more aggressive than other breeds, but with the proper upbringing they can make very dependable companions. You need to be able to read your dog.

Many factors contribute to aggression including genetics and environment. An improper environment, which may include the living conditions, lack of social life, excessive punishment, being attacked or frightened by an aggressive dog, etc., can all influence a dog's behavior. Even spoiling him and giving too much praise may be detrimental. Isolation and the lack of human contact or exposure to frequent teasing by children or adults also can ruin a good dog. Lack of direction, fear, or confusion lead to aggression in those dogs that are so inclined. Any obedience exercise, even the sit and down, can direct the dog and overcome fear and/or confusion. Every dog should learn these commands as a youngster, and there should be periodic reinforcement.

When a dog is showing signs of aggression, you should speak calmly (no screaming or hysterics) and firmly give a command that he understands, such as the sit. As soon as your dog obeys, you have assumed your dominant position. Aggression presents a problem because there may be danger to others. Sometimes it is an emotional issue. Owners may consciously or unconsciously encourage their dog's aggression. Other owners show responsibility by accepting the problem and taking measures to keep it under control. The owner is responsible for his dog's actions, and it is not wise to take a chance on someone being bitten, especially a child. Euthanasia is the solution for some owners and in severe cases this may be the best choice. However, few dogs are that dangerous and very few are that much of a threat to their owners. If caution is exercised and professional help is gained early on, most cases can be controlled.

Some authorities recommend feeding a lower protein (less than 20 percent) diet. They believe this can aid in reducing aggression. If the dog loses weight, then vegetable oil can be added. Veterinarians and behaviorists are having some success with pharmacology. In many cases treatment is possible and can improve the situation.

If you have done everything according to "the book" regarding training and socializing and are still having a behavior problem, don't procrastinate. It is important that the problem gets attention before it is out of hand. It is estimated that 20 percent of a veterinarian's time may be devoted to dealing with problems before they become so intolerable that the dog is separated from his home and owner. If your veterinarian isn't able to help, he should refer you to a behaviorist.

SUGGESTED READING

TS-143
*The Staffordshire Terriers
256 pages, over 250 full-
color photos*

RE-330
*The Guide to Owning a
Staffordshire Bull Terrier
64 pages, over 50 full-color
photos*

JG117
*A New Owner's Guide to
Dog Training
160 pages, 150 color
photos*

TS-258
*Training Your Dog for
Sports and Other Activities
160 pages, over 200 full-
color photos*

INDEX